I0014993

The OSINT Handbook

A practical guide to gathering and analyzing online information

Dale Meredith

The OSINT Handbook

Group Product Manager: Pavan Ramchandani

Publishing Product Manager: Prachi Sawant

Book Project Manager: Ashwin Kharwa

Senior Editor: Romy Dias

Technical Editor: Rajat Sharma

Copy Editor: Safis Editing

Proofreader: Romy Dias

Indexer: Subalakshmi Govindhan

Production Designer: Joshua Misquitta

DevRel Marketing Coordinator: Marylou De Mello

First published: March 2024

Production reference: 2230126

Published by Packt Publishing Ltd.

Grosvenor House

11 St Paul's Square

Birmingham

B3 1RB, UK.

ISBN 978-1-83763-827-7

www.packtpub.com

To Krista, "Daddy's Little Geek."

In the world of tech and cybersecurity, where I deal with complicated stuff like hacking and protecting computers, it's awesome to see you dive into technology just like me. You're not just my daughter; you're also my mini-me. Your excitement for all things tech makes our conversations so much fun and interesting.

This book is about my adventures in cybersecurity, but it's also a shout-out to you, for being into tech and always ready to learn something new. I hope you keep loving technology and exploring new ideas, just like you do now.

Love you lots,

Dad

Foreword

Gathering intelligence from the vast digital world stands as a cornerstone of effective defense. Within this complex domain lies Dale Meredith's latest work, a comprehensive exploration of **Open Source Intelligence (OSINT)**. In it, Dale delivers an indispensable guide for security professionals, investigators, and enthusiasts alike.

I've known Dale for nearly a decade as a colleague, fellow instructor, and friend. In that time, I've witnessed his unparalleled passion for cybersecurity. Dale's ability to make cyber concepts accessible and engaging is nothing short of remarkable. His work has illuminated the path for countless professionals, shaping the way we engage with our digital environment.

This book represents years of exploration, practice, and teaching in the field of OSINT. It's a testament to Dale's dedication to elevating the collective knowledge of the cybersecurity community. Dale extends in these pages an invitation into the depths of OSINT. He offers tools, techniques, and insights that are crucial for navigating the wealth of publicly available information that surrounds us.

What sets this work apart is Dale's ability to connect theory with practice. He bridges the gap between abstract concepts and real-world applications, ensuring that readers not only grasp the "how" but also the "why" behind OSINT methodologies. This book is not merely a manual but a narrative that captures the essence of OSINT, its challenges, and its potential to transform our approach to security.

Prepare to be challenged, enlightened, and ultimately empowered by this essential addition to your cybersecurity arsenal. Whether you're a seasoned practitioner or new to the field, Dale's exploration of OSINT offers valuable perspectives that will enrich your understanding and enhance your capabilities across the landscape of today's complex environments.

Greg Shields

Microsoft MVP and VMware vExpert

Contributors

About the author

Dale Meredith is an EC-Council-certified ethical hacker/instructor and a Microsoft-certified trainer. Dale has over 10 years of senior IT management experience and was a CTO for an ISP. Dale's skill as an IT trainer is in clarifying tough concepts and ensuring students understand the theory. Dale's teaching style is memorable and entertaining. His expertise has led to many opportunities, including teaching teams in Fortune 500 firms, universities globally, the Department of Homeland Security, and many US military branches. Along with authoring video courses, consulting, and classroom training, you can catch Dale on stage speaking at IT conferences around the world, helping teams keep their companies safe, relevant, and breach-aware.

To my wife, Alice Meredith. My concert buddy, my best friend, and my rock. Thanks for supporting me in my love of technology and building me up when things got rough.

A special thanks to the Packt Publishing team (Romy, Ashwin, Prachi, and I assume many others) for putting up with my busy schedule and being flexible when life got in my way.

To my grandkids. Thanks for letting me be Batman. "Everything's impossible until somebody does it."

– Bruce Wayne

About the reviewers

Deepanshu Khanna is an Indian Defense-appointed hacker and employed by the Indian government, Ministry of Home Affairs, police departments, and many other institutes, universities, globally renounced IT firms, magazines, and newspapers. He started his career by presenting a popular hack of GRUB at HATCON, as well as some of his popular research in the fields of IDS and AIDE. He practically showcased collisions in MD5 and buffer overflows, which was published in various magazines, including Pentestmag, Hackin9, eForensics, sd-journal, and Hack5. He has been invited to public conferences such as DEFCON, ToorCon, OWASP, HATCON, and H1hackz and various universities and institutes as a guest speaker.

Kalpa Kalhara Sampath is a distinguished academic and researcher in information security, computer malware, and artificial intelligence. He received a BSc in information technology, specializing in cybersecurity from the **Sri Lanka Institute of Information Technology (SLIIT)** and a master's in cybersecurity operations from the **University of New South Wales (UNSW)**. With over eight years of experience, he has significantly contributed to his field through numerous research papers and has been a dedicated lecturer and mentor in ethical hacking and digital forensics. His work continues to impact the academic community and beyond.

Table of Contents

1

The Secrets Hiding in Plain Sight – Unveiling the Power of OSINT   1

2

Invisible and Untouchable – The Importance of Anonymity in OSINT Analysis   11

5

From Recon-ng to Trace Labs – A Tour of the Best Open Source Intelligence Tools 97

6

The Eyes and Ears of Threat Intelligence – How OSINT Helps Mitigate Cyber Risks 131

7

Protecting Your Identity and Organization from Cyber Threats   151

8

Preface

You're about to embark on a fascinating journey into the realms of cybersecurity and **Open Source Intelligence** (**OSINT**). This book is designed to be your companion as you explore the intriguing world of digital information and how it can be harnessed for various purposes.

This book will introduce you to the basics of cybersecurity, from understanding the threats that exist online to learning how to safeguard your digital presence. You'll discover the importance of being vigilant in the digital world and how even the simplest actions can strengthen your defense against potential cyber attacks.

OSINT involves gathering information from publicly available sources, but it's more than just a Google search. You'll learn how to effectively locate and analyze information that's out in the open but is not always easy to find.

Who this book is for

This book is for anyone with a thirst for knowledge about the digital world, a desire to understand cybersecurity threats and defenses, and an interest in learning how to ethically gather and analyze publicly available information. Whether you're a student, a professional, or just someone fascinated by the digital world, this book will provide valuable insights and skills to help you navigate the complexities of cybersecurity and OSINT.

What this book covers

Chapter 1, The Secrets Hiding in Plain Sight – Unveiling the Power of OSINT, checks out what OSINT is all about. It's like being a detective on the internet, finding cool and important stuff that's out there for everyone to see. We'll see why OSINT is super useful today.

Chapter 2, Invisible and Untouchable – The Importance of Anonymity in OSINT Analysis, is where things get a bit sneaky. We talk about why it's important to keep yourself hidden (or anonymous) when you're looking up information. It's all about staying safe and not letting anyone know you're snooping around.

Chapter 3, The OSINT Toolbox – Methods and Techniques for Gathering and Analyzing Information, dives into the toolbox of OSINT. This means we'll look at all kinds of ways you can collect and understand information from the internet. Think of it as learning the tricks to be a smart online investigator.

Chapter 4, Exploring the Unknown – How Discovery Tools Reveal Hidden Information, is like going on a treasure hunt. We'll explore how special tools can help you find hidden or secret info online. It's about discovering things that aren't easy to find with a regular Google search.

Chapter 5, From Recon-ng to Trace Labs – A Tour of the Best Open Source Intelligence Tools, is like a tour of the best tools for OSINT. We'll check out cool programs and websites, such as Recon-ng and Tracelabs, and see how each of them can help you be a better digital detective.

Chapter 6, The Eyes and Ears of Threat Intelligence – How OSINT Helps Mitigate Cyber Risks, talks about how OSINT can be like having superpowers to protect against online dangers. This chapter shows how you can use OSINT to spot and stop cyber threats, keeping you and others safe on the internet.

Chapter 7, Protecting Your Identity and Organization from Cyber Threats, focuses on how to keep your info safe from the bad guys. We'll learn some awesome ways to protect yourself and your organization from cyber threats, using the cool stuff we've learned about OSINT.

Conventions used

There are a number of text conventions used throughout this book.

`Code in text`: Indicates code words in text, database table names, folder names, filenames, file extensions, pathnames, dummy URLs, user input, and Twitter handles. Here is an example: "The `inurl:` operator can help find URLs containing a specific keyword, sometimes leading to exposed directories or sensitive information."

A block of code is set as follows:

```
from bs4 import BeautifulSoup
import requests
response = requests.get('https://daledumbsitdown.com')
soup = BeautifulSoup(response.text, 'html.parser')
# Print the page title
print(soup.title.string)
```

When we wish to draw your attention to a particular part of a code block, the relevant lines or items are set in bold:

```
;; ANSWER SECTION:
host1234.examplehosting.com. 3600 IN A 93.184.216.34
site1.com. 3600 IN CNAME host1234.examplehosting.com.
site2.net. 3600 IN CNAME host1234.examplehosting.com.
site3.org. 3600 IN CNAME host1234.examplehosting.com.
```

Any command-line input or output is written as follows:

```
nslookup
> set type=MX
> daledumbsitdown.com
```

Bold: Indicates a new term, an important word, or words that you see onscreen. For instance, words in menus or dialog boxes appear in **bold**. Here is an example: "Right-click on communications streams and select **Follow TCP Stream** to reconstruct flows and uncover any readable packet data that may provide clues about function and purpose."

> **Tips or important notes**
> Appear like this.

Get in touch

Feedback from our readers is always welcome.

General feedback: If you have questions about any aspect of this book, email us at customercare@ packtpub.com and mention the book title in the subject of your message.

Errata: Although we have taken every care to ensure the accuracy of our content, mistakes do happen. If you have found a mistake in this book, we would be grateful if you would report this to us. Please visit www.packtpub.com/support/errata and fill in the form.

Piracy: If you come across any illegal copies of our works in any form on the internet, we would be grateful if you would provide us with the location address or website name. Please contact us at copyright@packt.com with a link to the material.

If you are interested in becoming an author: If there is a topic that you have expertise in and you are interested in either writing or contributing to a book, please visit authors.packtpub.com.

Free benefits with your book

This book comes with free benefits to support your learning. Activate them now for instant access (see the "*How to Unlock*" section for instructions).

Here's a quick overview of what you can instantly unlock with your purchase:

DRM-Free PDF Version

Download DRM-free PDF and ePub copies of this book.

7-Day Packt Library Access

Get 7-day unlimited access to 8,000+ books and videos. No credit card required.

Available for first-time Packt+ trial users only.

Next-Gen Reader Access

Read this book on Packt Reader with progress sync, dark mode and note-taking.

How to Unlock

Scan the QR code (or go to `packtpub.com/unlock`). Search for this book by name, confirm the edition, and then follow the steps on the page.

Note: Keep your invoice handy. Purchases made directly from Packt don't require one

Share your thoughts

Once you've read *The OSINT Handbook*, we'd love to hear your thoughts! Scan the QR code below to go straight to the Amazon review page for this book and share your feedback.

`https://packt.link/r/1837638276`

Your review is important to us and the tech community and will help us make sure we're delivering excellent quality content.

1

The Secrets Hiding in Plain Sight – Unveiling the Power of OSINT

Welcome to the fascinating and crazy world of **Open Source Intelligence (OSINT)**! As we kick off this chapter, get ready to unveil the hidden powers of OSINT, learn practical techniques, and discover the significant importance of OSINT in our digital world. After reading this chapter, you will be equipped with the necessary skills to expertly navigate the OSINT terrain.

In this chapter, we're going to cover the following main topics:

- Introduction to OSINT
- Passive and active OSINT
- Why OSINT matters in the digital age
- The OSINT framework
- Getting started with OSINT and some best practices

Throughout this chapter, I'll be your trusty dark knight, sharing hands-on examples and expert advice. You'll learn how to navigate the open source world, extract meaningful insights, and harness OSINT to achieve your goals. By the end, you'll possess a powerful set of skills that will give you a competitive edge, bolster your cybersecurity, and ensure you confidently navigate the vast digital frontier.

Are you ready to embark on this thrilling OSINT adventure? Let's get started and unlock the true potential of open source intelligence!

Your purchase includes a free PDF copy + exclusive extras

Your purchase includes a DRM-free PDF copy of this book, 7-day trial to the Packt+ library (no credit card required), and additional exclusive extras. See the *Free benefits with your book* section in the *Preface* to unlock them instantly and maximize your learning.

Introduction to OSINT

Open Source Intelligence, or **OSINT** as it's often called, can be understood as a process where we gather, evaluate, and make sense of information available in the public domain, all with the aim of answering a specific question related to intelligence.

Let's talk about information and intelligence

While they might appear similar at a glance, understanding the distinction between them is like learning the difference between raw ingredients and a finely cooked meal:

1. **Information: The starting point**

    Let's start with information. Think of it as the raw material. It's all around us, in various forms. Information is the tweets we read, the news articles we skim, and the countless posts that fill our social media feeds. It's abundant, varied, and its quality can range from top-notch to barely edible. In the OSINT world, this is where everything begins.

2. **Intelligence: The finished dish**

    Now, let's talk about intelligence. If information is the raw ingredient, intelligence is the full meal that's been carefully prepared and cooked. Intelligence comes from taking that raw information, analyzing it, understanding its context, and transforming it into something meaningful and useful. It's about making sense of the data, identifying patterns, drawing connections, and deriving insights that are relevant, specific, and, most importantly, actionable.

3. **The transformation process**

    The journey from raw information to refined intelligence is what OSINT is all about. It's a process that requires skill. It starts with collecting the right ingredients – in this case, gathering information from various open sources. Then comes the critical part: verifying the information, just as a chef would ensure the freshness of their ingredients.

4. **The analysis**

    Once we have verified information, the analysis begins. This is where the magic happens. We examine the information for patterns, look for anomalies, and try to understand the deeper story it tells. After analysis, we synthesize the information, combining the different pieces to form a comprehensive understanding, much like blending ingredients to create a perfect dish.

5. **Interpretation stage**

    Finally, there's the interpretation stage. We draw conclusions, understand the broader implications, and decide how this newly formed intelligence can guide decisions and strategies.

Passive and active OSINT

Let's chew the fat about the difference between passive and active OSINT. They're two sides of the same coin but can impact your organization in very different ways.

Passive OSINT is like being a ghost, watching the world but never interacting. You're digging through all the public info out there, but you're not engaging with anyone directly. No commenting on posts, no DMs, and definitely no friending or following. You're a fly on the wall, completely undetected.

On the flip side, active OSINT is getting stuck in, like, actually engaging with your target. Friending them on social platforms, commenting on their posts, or even shooting them a message. It's like being an undercover agent, and some places might even see it that way. Make sure you've got your boss's approval before you jump in with both feet.

If you plan on going the active route, you've got to blend in *like a ninja*. *"How Dale?"* Well, start by having a couple of different accounts on different platforms. This could help you look like a regular Joe.

Here's something to consider as well. Different organizations have different rules for what counts as passive or active. For example, joining a private Facebook group might seem like passive watching to some folks, while others might see it as getting involved. So, it's super important to know your organization's playbook on this.

Some folks argue that joining groups is still passive, as they're just there for the popcorn and not actually chatting with anyone.

Tricky, huh?

Why OSINT matters in the digital age

Right now, OSINT is being used by governments, businesses, non-profits, and other organizations. You'd be amazed at the applications, from sniffing out security threats, to market research, to competitive intelligence.

Here's a quick look at how OSINT is rocking the boat:

- **Academic research**: Researchers can use OSINT to grab data on all sorts of topics, such as social trends, public opinion, and economic indicators.
- **Business and market research**: Want to know what your competitors are up to, spot industry trends, or get a feel for consumer behavior? OSINT can do that, informing your business decisions and strategies.
- **Security and intelligence**: Think of OSINT as your personal Sherlock Holmes for threats such as terrorist activity or cyberattacks. It's also handy for keeping tabs on foreign governments, organizations, or criminal folks.

- **Investigative journalism**: Journalists can pull on the OSINT thread to unravel juicy stories in politics, business, crime, you name it.
- **Legal proceedings**: OSINT can play a big role in the courtroom, from gathering evidence to doing due diligence on potential witnesses or defendants.

Why is OSINT so cool?

The focus of OSINT is gathering public and legally accessible information. This eliminates the need to pursue classified or restricted sources, which can be costly and time-consuming.

It's great to know that OSINT offers a lot of sources to choose from, such as social media, news articles, government reports, and academic papers. This gives us a complete picture of various topics.

Another important consideration is timeliness. With the ability to gather OSINT in real time, you can stay up to date with the latest events and trends.

Another advantage of OSINT as a method of intelligence gathering is its cost-effectiveness. Unlike other methods such as human intelligence or signal intelligence, it doesn't require expensive equipment or specialized personnel, making it a more affordable option.

Finally, OSINT is incredibly transparent and easily verifiable. You can rely on the accuracy and reliability of the information you discover.

How the heck does OSINT work?

If you've ever wondered how the magic of open source intelligence happens, we're about to pull back the curtain for you:

1. **Collection**: Gather public info from various sources such as social media, news articles, government reports, academic papers, and commercial databases. You can do this manually or use automated tools.
2. **Processing**: Sift through the collected info to weed out duplicates, irrelevant data, or inaccurate stuff. It's all about filtering and categorizing based on relevance and importance.
3. **Analysis**: Take the processed info and spot trends, patterns, and relationships. Tools for data visualization, data mining, and natural language processing can really help here.
4. **Dissemination**: The final stage is sharing your findings with the decision-makers. This could be reports, briefings, or alerts, depending on what the organization needs.

The trick with OSINT is that it's a continuous cycle – you're always refining your collection, processing, and analysis based on new data and feedback. It's not a perfect science and shares the same limitations as other forms of intel collection. That's why it needs a keen eye and careful interpretation from trained analysts.

Lifting off the mask of OSINT, you're going to find a bunch of techniques for collecting and analyzing data. Let's summarize some of the sources:

- **Social media**: Platforms such as Twitter, Facebook, and LinkedIn are more than just online hangout spots. They're ripe for unearthing trends, gauging public sentiment, and sometimes flagging potential threats.

- **Web scraping**: This technique is like sending a modern-day prospector out into the digital wilderness. Specialized apps can extract a ton of data from websites quickly and systematically.

- **Search engines**: With good old search engines such as Google, you can use advanced search features (sometimes called Google-Dorking) to fine-tune your results and home in on the info you need.

- **Public records**: Think of public records as a chest of treasures, bursting with valuable information. Court documents, property records, and business filings can tell you a lot about individuals and organizations alike.

- **News sources**: Traditional news outlets such as newspapers and magazines, as well as online news sites, are a trove of insights. They can keep your finger on the pulse of current events, emerging trends, and potential issues of concern.

- **Data analysis tools**: When dealing with huge datasets, tools such as Excel, Tableau, and R are a godsend. They help sift through the noise and spotlight the patterns and relationships within the data.

Just remember, the OSINT landscape is extremely fluid. As new tech and data sources come into play, it's vital to stay on your toes and keep up with the latest methods and tools for effective OSINT gathering and analysis.

The OSINT framework

The Open Source Intelligence framework, widely known as OSINT framework (`https://osintframework.com/`), is a really cool resource for folks who are exploring open source intelligence. Think of it like a dynamic online catalog, housing a wealth of open source intelligence resources in a way that's easy to navigate and comprehend.

This handy tool is the brainchild of Justin Nordine, a well-respected figure in the cybersecurity landscape. He started the OSINT framework as a project to organize and share a plethora of online open source intelligence tools. As a testament to the spirit of collaboration in the cybersecurity field, it has morphed into a consistently updated, crowd-sourced platform that's widely used by security specialists across the globe.

When you visit the OSINT framework, you'll find that it's structured like an interactive mind map. You start with overarching categories, and as you click through, you can drill down into more specific resources and tools. This way, users can quickly find the resources they need, whether that's social media platforms, specialized search engines, databases with data leaks, government resources – you name it.

OSINT Framework

Figure 1.1 – The OSINT framework (https://osintframework.com/)

For professionals in the security industry, the OSINT framework is an absolute boon. It serves as an excellent starting point for the information-gathering and reconnaissance phase of any security assessment or investigation. By categorizing resources, the framework helps security experts pinpoint the best tools for their needs, thereby saving precious time during the research phase.

It's worth noting that the OSINT framework isn't a tool itself; it's more like a treasure map, guiding users to other valuable OSINT resources. As such, users should be mindful of how to use these individual tools properly and ethically, always keeping in mind the importance of respecting privacy and legal guidelines.

The beauty of the OSINT framework is in its simplicity and comprehensive scope. Plus, the regular updates ensure it remains a relevant reference for all professionals in the security industry, or anyone else interested in diving into open source intelligence. The OSINT framework is a shining example of the power of collaboration and open source work in the cybersecurity community.

Let's break down an investigation into some real-world examples

How about investigating the origin of a phishing email? Here's how:

1. **Initial analysis**: The recipient of the phishing email noticed suspicious elements and reported it to the relevant security team.

2. **Email metadata**: The email header was analyzed to extract metadata such as the sender IP address, timestamp, and routing information.

3. **IP address investigation**: The IP address was cross-referenced with publicly available OSINT sources, including domain registration databases, WHOIS records, and IP reputation services.

4. **Digital footprint analysis**: Social media platforms, online forums, and websites were scoured to identify any online presence associated with the IP address or related email addresses.

5. **Cross-source analysis**: Information gathered from different OSINT sources was combined and analyzed to establish connections and patterns.

6. **Attribution and reporting**: Based on the collected evidence, the investigators were able to identify the likely source of the phishing email. A comprehensive report was prepared, including all relevant details and recommendations for mitigating the threat.

What about using OSINT to trace the source of a data breach?

1. **Initial incident discovery**: An organization identifies a data breach through internal security measures or external reports.

2. **Gathering indicators**: Relevant indicators, such as leaked data samples or hacker aliases, are collected from the breached system or external sources.

    *   **Leaked data samples**: When a data breach occurs, attackers may often release a portion of the stolen data to prove their access and credibility. OSINT can be employed to search for these leaked data samples on various platforms. This could involve monitoring publicly accessible websites, forums, or dark web marketplaces where such data may be traded or shared. By leveraging OSINT tools and techniques, cybersecurity professionals can identify and analyze these samples to gain insights into the scope and nature of the breach.

    *   **Hacker aliases**: Cybercriminals often operate under various aliases or online personas. OSINT can be utilized to collect information about these aliases from different online sources, including social media platforms, forums, and chat channels. By conducting searches and analysis, cybersecurity professionals can uncover connections, patterns, or historical activities associated with these aliases. This information can help in establishing the identity or potential motives of the threat actors behind the breach.

    *   **Breached system analysis**: OSINT can also aid in gathering indicators directly from the compromised system itself. By examining system logs, network traffic, or other digital artifacts, cybersecurity professionals can identify traces left behind by the attackers. These indicators may include IP addresses, **command and control** (**C2**) infrastructure, malware signatures, or other technical artifacts that can provide valuable insights into the breach. OSINT tools and techniques can assist in cross-referencing these indicators with publicly available sources to uncover any relevant information about the attackers or their method.

3. **Dark web monitoring**: OSINT tools are employed to monitor underground forums, marketplaces, and chat channels on the dark web to search for any mentions of the breached data or related activities.

4. **Social media monitoring**: Publicly accessible social media platforms are monitored for any discussions, posts, or comments that might provide insights into the breach or the perpetrators.

5. **Analysis of leaked data**: If any portions of the breached data are publicly available, OSINT techniques are utilized to analyze its content, including usernames, email addresses, or any identifying information that could aid in the investigation.

6. **Attribution and collaboration**: The collected OSINT findings are shared with relevant law enforcement agencies, cybersecurity firms, or industry-specific organizations to collaborate on the investigation.

7. **Legal action or mitigation**: Based on the identified source and evidence, appropriate legal actions or mitigation measures are taken to minimize the impact of the data breach and prevent future incidents.

So now, maybe you're getting a better idea of how OSINT can benefit you and your organization.

Getting started with OSINT and some best practices

OSINT can be exciting, offering valuable information and investigative possibilities. Here are some practical tips, helpful insights, and recommended resources to help you begin your OSINT adventure and build a solid foundation in research.

Tips and tricks for effective information gathering

When it comes to gathering intel, define your goals and what you hope to achieve. This will help you maintain focus and streamline your research efforts. Before delving into the vast expanse of information that, trust me, you'll be presented with, develop a structured methodology.

Break down your investigation into logical steps, ensuring you cover all relevant aspects. Utilize a range of sources for information gathering. This can include search engines, social media platforms, public records, government websites, specialized OSINT tools, and more. Verifying information from multiple sources enhances accuracy and minimizes the risk of misinformation.

Enhance your skills in crafting effective search queries. Familiarize yourself with operators, filters, and advanced search features provided by search engines to narrow down results and locate specific information.

Explore metadata associated with digital files, images, and documents. Analyzing metadata can provide valuable insights, such as location details, timestamps, author information, or device specifics.

Here's one for you: learn to follow digital footprints. This involves investigating social media profiles, online forums, blog posts, and publicly available records to gain a comprehensive understanding of your subject. Don't worry, I'll show you how to do this later.

Maintain detailed records of your findings, including timestamps, URLs, screenshots, and relevant notes. Organizing your research facilitates efficient analysis and allows easy reference to information when needed.

Some resources we'll be using

From conducting background checks on job candidates to identifying potentially risky websites, popular OSINT tools empower users to gather the necessary information for their specific needs. By adding these tools to your utility-belt, you'll be able to streamline your research process and uncover valuable insights that aid in decision-making. Remember, the power of OSINT lies in its ability to harness publicly accessible data and transform it into meaningful intelligence. Here's *Dale's Top 12* list of tools we'll be working with:

- Maltego: `https://www.maltego.com/`
- SpiderFoot: `https://intel471.com/solutions/attack-surface-protection`
- Intelligence X: `https://intelx.io/`
- Shodan: `https://www.shodan.io/`
- OSINT Framework: `https://osintframework.com/`
- Metagoofil: `https://github.com/opsdisk/metagoofil`
- Lampyre: `https://lampyre.io/`
- Spokeo: `https://www.spokeo.com/`
- Recon-ng: `https://github.com/lanmaster53/recon-ng`
- Mitaka: `https://github.com/ninoseki/mitaka`
- Babel Street: `https://www.babelstreet.com/`
- Seon: `https://seon.io/`

> **Sidebar**
>
> I talked about the OSINT framework earlier. This site (`https://osintframework.com/`) is extremely fluid and will provide us with a plethora of websites and tools as well. Trust me, we'll reference it a lot within this book.

Summary

We started on OSINT and why it's become such a big deal. We also learned why it's such a big deal nowadays. Like any superpower (tool), it can be used for good or evil, plus there's a right way and a wrong way to use OSINT. We talked about some best practices to ensure you're gathering and using information responsibly and ethically. No cybersecurity hero ever succeeded by being sloppy, after all!

Then we rolled up our sleeves and got into the real stuff – actual examples of OSINT at work. We looked at how it can help sniff out phishing scams, or how it could be used to investigate data breaches!

Finally, we set you up with some handy tips and resources to help you prepare for an OSINT engagement. Think of it as the starter pack for your OSINT utility belt.

So, that's *Chapter 1* in a nutshell. It's a sturdy launching pad into the realm of OSINT. Up next, we'll talk about the methods and techniques for gathering OSINT.

Get this book's PDF version and more

Scan the QR code (or go to `packtpub.com/unlock`). Search for this book by name, confirm the edition, and then follow the steps on the page.

Note: Keep your invoice handy. Purchases made directly from Packt don't require an invoice.

Invisible and Untouchable – The Importance of Anonymity in OSINT Analysis

In the dynamic field of **Open Source Intelligence (OSINT)**, safeguarding one's anonymity isn't just a best practice; it's a vital component of effective research. This chapter aims to shed light on anonymity's critical role in OSINT analysis. As we navigate through various sections, we will emphasize the significance of protecting personal privacy while conducting comprehensive intelligence gathering. By the end of this chapter, you will be equipped with the knowledge and skills necessary to maintain anonymity, manage your digital footprint, and communicate securely during the OSINT examination.

We will cover the following main topics in this chapter:

- Introduction to anonymity and privacy in OSINT
- Protecting your digital footprint
- Staying ahead of cyber threats

Introduction to anonymity and privacy in OSINT

OSINT research involves the data mining of openly available resources. However, OSINT analysts must take precautions to preserve their privacy and anonymity for many important reasons, including the following:

- **Avoid tipping off subjects**: If individuals or organizations become aware they are being investigated through OSINT, they may act to prevent data collection. They could delete social media posts, restrict profile visibility, take websites offline, or even destroy evidence. Maintaining anonymity is crucial to avoiding alerting subjects to monitoring.

- **Prevent compromising operations**: Similarly, if targets realize they are being watched, they may change their activities or communications to avoid further detection. This could severely disrupt ongoing OSINT operations before investigators have gathered enough actionable intelligence. Anonymity helps avoid operations being exposed.

- **Stop illicit activities from continuing**: If investigations are compromised early on, law enforcement and other agencies may be unable to identify criminal conspiracies or gather the evidence needed to prosecute illegal activities. Subjects could continue operations under the radar. Anonymity is key to thoroughly monitoring subjects without detection.

- **Avoid legal and ethical issues**: In some states/countries, tipping off subjects about an investigation can lead to criminal charges. Anonymity helps avoid inadvertent ethical and legal violations.

- **Protect analysts and sources**: Threat actors such as hackers, terrorists, and criminal networks could retaliate against analysts and sources who they discover are investigating them. Anonymity and privacy safeguards help keep us analysts and our sources safe.

- **Prevent data breaches**: Sensitive information must be protected from falling into the wrong hands, and this can only be done with rigorous data handling and access controls. In order to avoid catastrophic data leaks, secure privacy practices must be in place.

Ways anonymity can be breached in OSINT

So, how can you be detected during an investigation? Well, let's take a look at several methods:

- **IP address exposure**: One of the easiest ways you can hide yourself is via your IP address. If you're not using a VPN or Tor, your real IP address will be logged by the websites you visit.

  As a cybersecurity researcher, I once faced a daunting challenge. I needed to uncover information about cyberattacks that seemed to originate from a specific area. To do this without alerting the attackers, I turned to a **Virtual Private Network (VPN)**. I connected to a server in a different country, which hid my real IP address and location. It appeared as if I was browsing from that server's location, not my own. This allowed me to safely explore various websites and forums, gathering the information I needed without exposing my identity. This experience taught me the power of a VPN in protecting one's digital presence, especially when researching sensitive topics.

- **Browser fingerprinting**: Web browsers collect a surprising amount of data, from screen resolution to installed plugins, which can be used to create a unique *fingerprint*. Don't believe me? Take a break and head over to `privacy.net/analyzer`. See, I told you!

What information can a website find out about you when you visit it? A lot more than you probably realize. This tool lists information that any website, advertisement, and widget can collect from your web browser. Such information could be used to identify you and/or track your behavior using tactics like IP lookups and browser fingerprinting. While none of this may be considered personally identifiable information (P the profile drawn from all these pieces of information can be so distinct that it can only plausibly match a single person.

Tests

This page includes several tests that you can scroll through and perform one at a time to evaluate your browser privacy.

PLEASE NOTE: In order to demonstrate that a malicious site can easily detect logged in accounts without asking your permission, this tool ' contact 30 popular websites where you may be logged in. However we don't access these sites but simply present them as potential risks to your privacy.

1. Basic Info   2. Autofill Leak Test   3. User Account Tests   4. Browser Capability Test   5. Fingerprint analysis

Basic Info

You are using a Laptop or Desktop running Win32 OS. **Your browser is Chrome 119 and resolution is set to 1285x1309.** Your Laptop or Desktop has 100% battery remaining.

Figure 2.1 – My results on privacy.net/analyzer

Oh, and if you think incognito mode will protect you, nope. Browser fingerprinting can still track your activities across different sessions.

- **Overconfidence in technology**: Relying solely on tools such as VPNs and Tor without fully understanding their limitations can create a false sense of security. For example, some VPN services actually log user activity, IPs, timestamps, etc., despite marketing claims of being *no-logs* services. Tor traffic can be de-anonymized in some cases by powerful adversaries such as government agencies. No single technology is a silver bullet when it comes to anonymity. You need to layer different protections and be cognizant of the weak points in each tool or approach.

- **Cookie tracking**: Cookies are small text files that websites place on your device to track and remember your online activity. While cookies can be convenient for things such as remembering login info or shopping cart contents, they also allow companies to build detailed profiles about your browsing habits, interests, behaviors, and much more across multiple sites and sessions. Regularly clearing your cookies can help limit tracking, but companies have developed more advanced techniques such as browser fingerprinting and canvas fingerprinting that don't rely on cookies to track you. Using privacy-focused browsers such as Tor and covering your online tracks by avoiding behavior patterns are important ways to avoid surveillance.

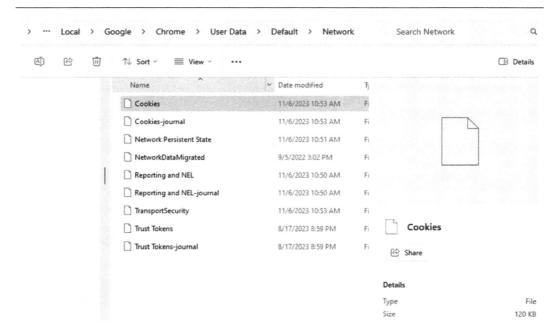

Figure 2.2 – Cookies are stored in different locations, but can expose quite a bit of intel

- **Metadata leaks**: Files such as documents, photos, audio, and video recordings all contain metadata—information generated by your device about the file itself. This can include geotags, time stamps, device serial numbers, editing history, and more. Similarly, communications such as emails have headers that reveal your IP address, client info, etc. If this metadata leaks, it can reveal details about your identity and compromise your anonymity. You need to be very careful about stripping metadata from files before publishing them, using metadata removal tools. Avoiding communication methods that expose metadata is also important.

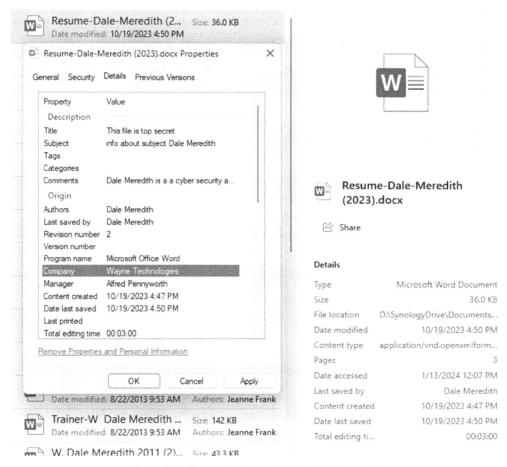

Figure 2.3 – Example of metadata included on a file

- **Insecure public Wi-Fi**: Public Wi-Fi networks at coffee shops, airports, hotels, etc. often have no password or security measures at all. This allows anyone nearby to easily intercept the unencrypted traffic passing through the network and eavesdrop on your Internet activity. Never access any sensitive accounts such as emails, banking apps, or confidential data while on insecure public Wi-Fi. Always use a trusted VPN on public networks to encrypt your traffic. Better yet, avoid transmitting sensitive data until you are on a known secure network again.

- **Social engineering**: Despite advancing technical protections, human nature remains vulnerable to old-fashioned social engineering attacks such as phishing. Avoiding password reuse across accounts, enabling multi-factor authentication wherever possible, establishing PGP-encrypted contacts, and training yourself to cautiously identify potential scams before clicking links or attachments is critical. No anonymity toolkit can protect against you being tricked into giving up personal information.

- **Personal accounts for OSINT**: One of the worst OPSEC mistakes you can make is to conduct OSINT investigations and cybersecurity research from accounts that can be traced back to your real identity. Always use anonymous, disposable accounts and masked IP addresses when gathering intelligence via search engines, social networks, forums, and other online venues. Maintain strict separation between your personal online presence and investigative online presence.

- **Accidental slip-ups**: A single accidental leak of personal information in a chat room, forum post, or conversation app can be enough to shatter your anonymity. Be extremely cautious when sharing any details about yourself online that could help identify you. Also, be consistent about separating your anonymous personas—reusing usernames, email patterns, passwords, etc. across accounts makes it easier to correlate your activity. A momentary lapse of vigilance is all it takes.

- **Outdated knowledge**: New hacking techniques, exploits, and vulnerabilities are emerging all the time. If you don't continuously educate yourself about the latest privacy and security threats, your information could be snatched by new methods you're unaware of and haven't protected yourself against yet. You can never assume your current knowledge is sufficient—learning needs to be an ongoing process to keep up with an evolving threat landscape. Relying too much on technology such as VPNs or Tor without understanding their limitations can give you a false sense of security. For instance, some VPN services log user activity, and Tor is not immune to all forms of tracking.

Striking the balance – Privacy concerns in OSINT investigations

Look, tech has always been a game-changer, "*Duh, Dale*"! While it's awesome for nabbing criminals, villains, and arch-enemies, it can also slice right through our personal privacy if we're not careful.

We need a system where there's oversight, checks, balances, and—most importantly—accountability. We can't just let these powerful tools run wild without some ground rules. And hey, these rules need to be transparent so that you and I can have a say if something doesn't smell right.

Technology itself doesn't have a moral compass; it's just a tool. We've got to be smart, ethical, and, above all, vigilant. In the end, it's all about the long game. If we sacrifice our principles for some short-term security wins, we're setting ourselves up for some serious long-term losses. We've got to keep our eyes on the prize: a society that's both safe and free. And that, my friends, is a balancing act worth perfecting. OK, I think you get my point, I'll get off my soapbox.

Protecting your digital footprint

Your digital footprint is like your shadow on a sunny day—always there, slightly altering its form as you move through life. Yet, this shadow can often expose more than we'd care to reveal. Your personal information, such as your home address or social security number, is merely a click away from prying eyes. Now let's get something straight; you didn't sign up for this level of exposure. But it's happening, and we should all be alarmed.

Managing and limiting YOUR online presence

Before we get into performing an OSINT investigation on a target, it is important for us as security professionals to understand methods of protecting ourselves. Did you know that approximately 91% of cybercrimes start with a simple email? (`https://www.yeoandyeo.com/resource/91-of-cyberattacks-begin-with-a-phishing-email.`)

It's possible for an attacker to not know your name at first. However, with more data, they can eventually build a complete picture of your digital identity. In today's world, data is as valuable as oil. Recognizing how simple it is for someone to obtain your information is not only concerning, but it's also a call to action.

Your personal data is being exploited by cybercriminals, stalkers, and profit-driven corporations. Although you may not be directly selling your information, your daily online activities are doing it for you. Every Google search you make, every social media post you publish, and even every product you browse on an e-commerce website contribute to a complete profile of you—one that you didn't even create.

Figure 2.4 – Google tracks you with your phone (https://timeline.google.com/)

Why protecting personal data is more important than ever

Digital data vulnerability isn't merely about the *now*. It has far-reaching consequences, including identity theft and even personal safety risks. The impact is multidimensional. For instance, an imposter using your identity could apply for loans, make illegal transactions, or even conduct criminal activities. Clearing your name afterward is not only an enormous task, but it can be financially and emotionally draining.

Data vulnerability can have a significant impact on your personal life as well. For example, a potential employer may come across inaccurate or unfavorable information about you, which could damage your reputation before you even have a chance to demonstrate your abilities.

The stakes are high and the odds, unfortunately, are not in your favor. However, don't resign to digital fate just yet. Let me give you some tips for being not just digitally aware but also digitally empowered. Your personal information is precious; it's time to start treating it that way.

Internet browsers – The frontline of data vulnerability

The browser is your friendly digital conduit that gets you from here to there on the information superhighway. It's where you read the news, watch videos, engage in social media warfare, and what have you. However, lurking underneath that user-friendly interface is a data-collection apparatus that puts the NSA to shame. No, I'm not here to fill your head with conspiracy theories. But remember my saying: "*Just because I don't see the black helicopters doesn't mean they aren't there!*"

First-party vs. third-party cookies

Yep, there are different types of cookies to fill our browser's tummies:

- **First-party cookies**: Stored by the website you're visiting. They remember your settings, what's in your shopping cart, and more.
- **Third-party cookies**: Stored by someone other than the website you're on, often advertisers. These are the cookies that follow you around the web, serving up that pair of shoes you glanced at once but didn't buy.

Enter the cookie grabber

This tool, known as a cookie grabber, is designed to snatch those cookies. The danger? It can grab both types of cookies, even those with sensitive info such as your login details.

For instance, you visit a site with an embedded cookie grabber. Without a hint of suspicion, you log in, and just like that, your session cookies are stolen. Now, the attacker has a key to your digital kingdom and access to your accounts on other platforms, all from a simple, unnoticed theft.

It gets more unsettling. Let's talk about websites that store your credentials—your usernames and passwords—in plain text right in your browser. It sounds technical, but here's the deal: sometimes, when you log into a site, it keeps a record of your login details in a format anyone can read. If your computer is compromised or you're on a shared computer, someone could use a basic tool, such as a hex editor, to see these credentials. It's like leaving your house keys on a park bench and walking away.

Imagine logging into a website that doesn't take your privacy seriously. Your credentials are stored in plain text in a cookie. You're none the wiser, but a hacker or even a nosy roommate could extract this information with ease, breaking into your accounts as if they were their own:

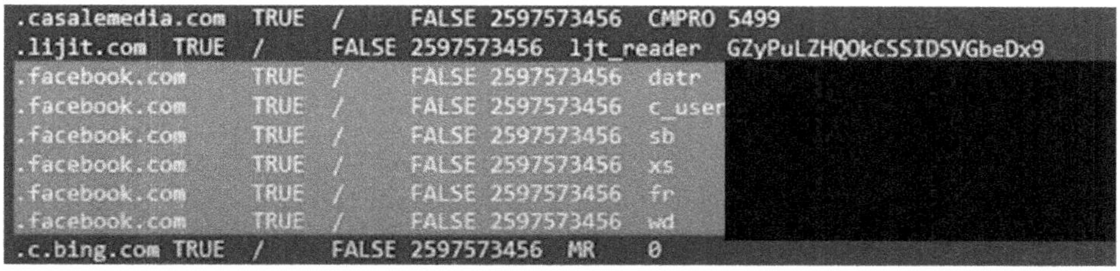

```
.casalemedia.com  TRUE  /      FALSE 2597573456  CMPRO    5499
.1ijit.com  TRUE  /      FALSE 2597573456  ljt_reader  GZyPuLZHQOkCSSIDSVGbeDx9
.facebook.com       TRUE  /     FALSE 2597573456  datr
.facebook.com       TRUE  /     FALSE 2597573456  c_user
.facebook.com       TRUE  /     FALSE 2597573456  sb
.facebook.com       TRUE  /     FALSE 2597573456  xs
.facebook.com       TRUE  /     FALSE 2597573456  fr
.facebook.com       TRUE  /     FALSE 2597573456  wd
.c.bing.com  TRUE  /      FALSE 2597573456  MR       0
```

Figure 2.5 – Using a cookie grabber, you can assume someone's account or identity

How to protect yourself

Both VPNs and proxy chains serve as effective tools for maintaining online privacy. They help in obscuring your real IP address, making it difficult for third-party cookies to track your internet activities. This is especially valuable in today's digital world, where online tracking and data privacy are major concerns. However, it's important to choose reputable VPN and proxy services, as they have access to your internet data. Always prioritize services that are known for their strong privacy policies and commitment to user security.

DuckDuckGo: the unsung hero of privacy-focused browsing

If mainstream browsers are the attention-seeking reality TV stars of the digital world, DuckDuckGo is the introverted genius no one's heard of but should have. DuckDuckGo is on a mission to simplify online privacy. The plucky company blocks hidden trackers that follow you around the web. Their software firewall shuts down attempts to collect your search history and personal information.

DuckDuckGo's products are entirely focused on giving you control over your data. Their search engine never stores search history or user information. All searches are private by default. The browser extension and mobile app also block invasive trackers lurking on websites.

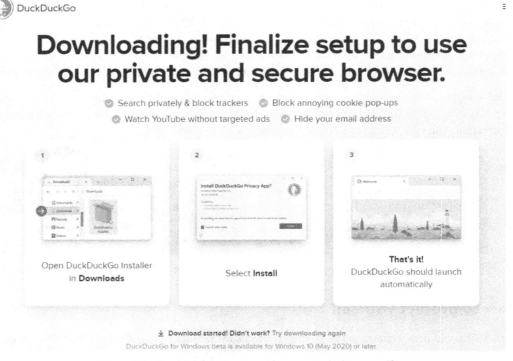

Figure 2.6 – DuckDuckGo is a great browser to hide yourself

Encryption provides another layer of protection by securing connections between you and websites. Together, these tools form an effective privacy shield to stop advertising companies and other third parties from profiling you.

DuckDuckGo makes money by showing keyword-based ads instead of creepy targeted ones, so they have no need to create personal data profiles. Their business aligns with their mission to put privacy first.

So, you're ready to make the switch? Excellent. But you can't just storm out of one relationship and into another without some prep. Here's how to do it:

1. **Download and install**: Get your chosen privacy-focused browser.

2. **Import settings**: Most browsers will allow you to import bookmarks and settings from your old browser.

3. **Set as default**: Make your new browser the go-to for all your digital escapades.

Browser alternatives: pros and cons of other private browsers

Now, let's not romanticize DuckDuckGo as the only superhero here. There are other options too, each with its own set of perks and quirks.

Brave browser

This is one browser I recommend to everyone. It's kind of the new kid on the block

The privacy-centric Brave browser (`https://brave.com/`) is an excellent starting point for obscuring your online activity. Brave blocks trackers by default, reducing the ability of third parties to monitor you.

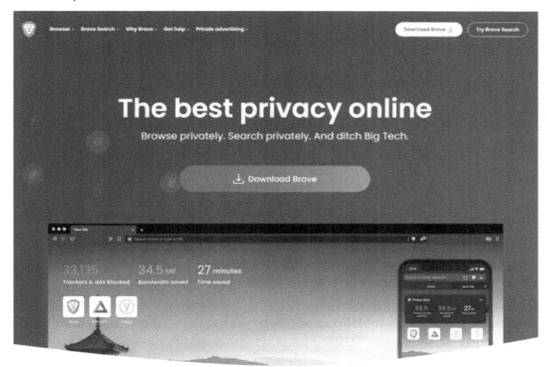

Figure 2.7 – Brave is my personal choice for hiding my identity

For those wary of switching browsers, extensions such as Startpage offer similar protections.

Startpage displays a privacy score between one and five so you can see just how many trackers and cookies it foiled on each site. The details may shock you, but will ultimately empower you. Startpage also cloaks your identity from any trackers that do run by masking your digital fingerprint.

Figure 2.8 – The Startpage extension is available in the Chrome web store

While blocking trackers, you may need to permit certain benign cookies so sites function properly. Startpage allows you to approve cookies individually—no need for blanket access. For searches, Startpage queries Google anonymously so they can't add to your creepy profile.

Between Brave's robust protections and Startpage's actionable insights, you now have potent weapons to evaporate your digital shadow. No longer will you be passive prey to cyberstalking trackers. The following are its pros and cons:

- **Pros**: It blocks ads and trackers by default
- **Cons**: The built-in ad system might not be everyone's cup of tea

Tor browser

Tor (or The Onion Router) is a networked community united by a common cause—online privacy. Tor was born from rebellion. While governments spy and corporations track, Tor fights back. It's an online resistance movement, with servers, relays, and nodes, run by volunteers worldwide. No single point can trace the full path.

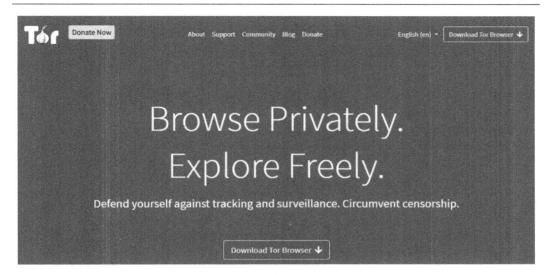

Figure 2.9 – The Tor website

Tor scrubs metadata and masks IP addresses. Traffic is encrypted and re-encrypted as it hops through the privacy network. Like peeling back layers of an onion, each relay only knows the next stop, not the final destination.

This is only possible through strength in numbers. Thousands of selfless volunteers lend their computers as Tor nodes. These diverse entry, middle, and exit points form the decentralized backbone of the network. Censorship-resistant connections sealed with privacy-protecting encryption.

Tor is free software (`https://torproject.org`) built by a community of believers. The code is open for all to inspect and improve. Transparency keeps Tor true to its mission. There are no shady backdoors or hidden agendas baked into the tools. The following are its pros and cons:

- **Pros**: Tor offers the highest level of anonymity
- **Cons**: It has a slower browsing speed due to multiple server hops

But Dale, what browsers would you stay away from? Well, folks, that list goes a little like this (in no particular order):

- Google Chrome
- Microsoft's Edge
- Firefox
- Opera
- Safari

Your browser is your first line of defense against cyber threats. It's more than just a gateway to the internet; it's the fortress that guards your data with solid power. Make the change and fortify your browser today. Your digital self will be grateful for the extra protection.

Creating and managing online personas – Sock puppets

Now, before your imagination runs wild, no, we're not talking about crafting a delightful puppet out of your favorite pair of socks. Sock puppets are fictitious online identities created for the purposes of deception, manipulation, or information gathering. Like puppets on an entertainer's hand, they are characters that allow the puppeteer to take on a different persona and interact incognito.

While not inherently illegal, sock puppets are often frowned upon due to their capacity for abuse. They can be used to spread misinformation, artificially boost popularity, harass others anonymously, or infiltrate communities under false pretenses. However, they also have legitimate uses in fields such as investigative journalism or penetration testing.

There are several motivations for individuals and organizations to use sock puppet accounts:

- **Anonymity**: The primary purpose is to dissociate online activities from one's true identity. This anonymity facilitates information gathering without revealing oneself.
- **Deception**: Sock puppets allow one to influence conversations, share false information, and manipulate perceptions. This deceptive capacity can be used for infiltration or social engineering.
- **Reconnaissance**: They are effective tools for gathering intelligence about people, organizations, topics of interest, etc. without detection.
- **Privacy**: Some may simply want to protect their privacy by separating their online presence into multiple unconnected identities.

Setting the stage: creating your sock puppet

An online persona created for the purposes of anonymity and information gathering can be a powerful tool when applied ethically. Sock puppets serve as digital chameleons, blending into the online environment to collect open source intelligence without revealing the investigator's true identity. This practice is particularly valuable in scenarios where revealing one's identity may skew the information obtained or pose a risk to the investigator's safety.

Imagine, for example, a cybersecurity expert tasked with assessing the security of a financial institution. By ethically deploying a sock puppet, they can interact with suspect phishing sites or malicious actors to understand their tactics—without exposing the institution or themselves to undue risk. It's a bit like an undercover cop in the digital neighborhood, watching and learning but not interfering.

Additionally, sock puppets can play a crucial role in tracking cyber threats. They can be used to monitor dark web forums or infiltrate cybercriminal networks, gathering intelligence on emerging threats, data breaches, or the sale of stolen data. This allows cybersecurity professionals to warn potential victims and fortify defenses before any actual harm is done.

The ethical use of sock puppets in OSINT is underpinned by a strict code of conduct: they are not used for deception or manipulation, but rather as a shield to protect the identity of the security professional while they gather the necessary intelligence to bolster our digital defenses. It's a cloak of invisibility for the good guys, allowing them to observe and report without becoming targets themselves.

Here are some things to consider when creating your sock puppet:

- Clearly define the purpose of your sock puppet. It could be for research, data collection, or cybersecurity exercises. Always have a clear and ethical goal in mind.

- Creating a sock puppet starts with crafting a believable persona. Kind of like building a character for a play, you'll need a backstory, interests, and even quirks. Tools such as the Fake Name Generator (`https://www.fakenamegenerator.com/`) or NameFake (`https://namefake.com/`) can be your best pals here, helping you come up with a genuine-sounding identity.

    Expand beyond just a name to create an identity, including the following:

    - Date and place of birth

    - Hometown

    - Education and work history

    - Interests and hobbies

    - Favorite books, movies, music

    - Political views

    - Religion

    - Photos and images

    Some will call these steps pretexting.

> **Note**
> Oh, is that a new word for you? Well, what I mean by pretexting is not just pretending to be someone else; you're creating a whole backstory, setting, and script to make it believable.

- You'll want to have an image/photograph of your persona to make your puppet look as real as possible. A website called `https://thispersondoesnotexist.com/` does a great job of using completely AI (artificial intelligence) generated images of folks. This way, someone can't do a reverse image search to find out that you just borrowed someone else's photo.

Figure 2.10 – Yep, this isn't anyone in real life; it's AI-generated (https://thispersondoesnotexist.com)

- You'll want to set up a dedicated email account for your persona. You can you a service such as 20 Minute Mail (`https://www.20minutemail.com/`).

- Set up some accounts and profiles on social platforms for your sock puppet.

> **Note**
>
> Remember, the key to a great performance is consistency, so maintain the same persona across different platforms

- Utilize VPNs (such as `https://www.expressvpn.com/`) to mask your IP address and consider using browsers that prioritize user privacy, such as Tor (`https://www.torproject.org/`), to keep your real identity hidden behind the curtain.

I was once interviewed by a reporter. I preferred to keep my anonymity. I chose to use Tor, which encrypts internet traffic by routing it through several servers worldwide. Along with an encrypted messaging service found on the dark web, I was able to communicate with this reporter securely. Our discussions were completely private, with no risk of being traced back to us. Don't forget to give your puppet a phone number! Using a service such as TextFree (`https://textfree.us/`), you can send and receive text messages without exposing your real number. It's kind of cool.

Setting up anonymous communication

To prevent sock puppet accounts from being linked back to their creators, anonymous communication channels are essential. This involves creating untraceable email addresses and burner phones.

When setting up the puppet's email account, consider the following:

- Avoid unusual providers that raise red flags

- Use common services such as Gmail or Outlook

- Create the address through public Wi-Fi or a VPN to remain anonymous

- Ensure the name sounds realistic and doesn't just use random characters

- The email will be used for registering accounts, so anonymity is key

Burner phones are clutch for keeping your investigation on the down low, but you have to use them carefully. Only use a burner for stuff directly tied to your case—calls, texts, 2FA codes, etc.

Figure 2.11 – Some of my personal burners I've used for engagements

Never ever save sensitive docs, names, dates, locations, or other case details on the device. Remember, burners can still get tapped, hacked, or compromised despite being disposable. So, take extra precautions such as using encrypted chat apps (Signal and WhatsApp), not linking the burner to personal accounts, turning off GPS, removing metadata from pics, and regularly clearing caches. Use code names when contacting sources instead of real ones.

When conducting an OSINT investigation, the responsible management of burner devices is a crucial step in the operation's lifecycle. When an investigation concludes or if there's a suspicion that the integrity of a burner has been compromised, it's time to ensure that the device is retired securely and professionally. You'll want to take one of two steps in handling these devices:

- **Archive the device responsibly**: This is akin to how sensitive materials are handled post-operation—maintaining a clear chain of custody. By securely storing the burner with the client, alongside any other used equipment, we ensure that all resources, data, and potential evidence remain intact and under proper oversight. This practice isn't about hoarding hardware—it's about the meticulous separation of duties and maintaining an unimpeachable professional standard.

- **Have a meticulous decommissioning process**: Begin with a thorough factory reset to erase all data, a standard procedure in the industry. Then, physically disassemble the device. Removing and rendering the SIM card unusable is essential—this may involve cutting it into pieces, a method endorsed by security protocols to prevent data recovery. Deconstructing the device further—separating the screen from the battery, for example—is a measure taken to ensure that no recoverable component falls into the wrong hands. Disposal should be executed with discretion and distributed across various locations to mitigate the risk of data reconstruction.

These measures aren't the cloak-and-dagger tactics of a crime drama; they're the bread and butter of ethical hacking and professional digital investigation. A burner phone is a shield, safeguarding both the investigator's anonymity and the integrity of their work. Employing these devices, with their eventual disposal, is a testament to a professional's commitment to security and confidentiality in a field where the stakes are invariably high.

Remember, every step we take is geared toward strengthening security postures and uncovering vulnerabilities before they can be exploited maliciously. Our practices are transparent to clients and within legal bounds, ensuring that our work always aligns with the noble goal of protecting assets and information in a world increasingly reliant on digital infrastructures.

By keeping communication anonymous, there will be no way to connect sock puppets to their creators. The accounts will appear entirely self-contained.

Maintaining anonymity is crucial when creating sock puppet accounts in order to preserve privacy and enable deception. Untraceable communication channels are essential to this goal.

Pulling the strings – Operating your sock puppet

Now that your puppet is ready to grace the cyber stage, it's important to follow some ethical guidelines:

- **Transparency with stakeholders**: If you're using sock puppets for research or corporate exercises, maintain transparency with stakeholders about your methods and intentions.

- **Data protection**: Be a guardian of data protection. Collect only the data necessary for your research and handle it with the utmost responsibility.

- **Documentation and reporting**: Keep meticulous records of your puppet's activities. This not only helps in presenting your findings but also ensures accountability.

Leveraging gender dynamics in sock puppet operations

When diving into the cyber investigative scene, piecing together your online alter ego is part art, part science, and all about walking that ethical tightrope, especially when it comes to gender dynamics in the digital world. Yes, the internet's chock-full of gender stereotypes, but when we're crafting these personas, we've got to handle them with care.

Imagine you choose to use a female character for your online disguise. It's true that being a woman might help in some situations because of how people have always interacted socially. But remember, we're not here to trick people just for the sake of it. We're smart about how we do things, not sneaky. The real point is that you can use smart moves such as the honeypot method, where you might act a bit flirty and vulnerable to get your target's attention. But doing this means you have to be really careful about staying ethical. It's about gathering information in a clever way, not misleading or using people.

When it comes to making your sock puppet believable, the devil's in the details. Skip the stereotype rehash and give your digital decoy some real personality. A dash of unique flair makes your puppet more than just a bunch of pixels—it becomes a believable character that can gain trust where it's needed most.

> **Note**
>
> Here's a pro tip: keep your sock puppet on a completely different leash from your real online life. Think virtual machines, sandboxed browsers—the works. Mixing the two is like wearing socks with sandals; it just doesn't look right. This is how you keep your cover story tight and your real identity under wraps.

These sock puppet shenanigans have their place on the right side of the cyber tracks. They're dynamite for infiltrating shady online groups to sniff out security risks or pretending to be a greenhorn in your own company to see who bites the bait in a phishing test. It's all about putting those cybersecurity hats on and using our powers for the good guys.

So, let's keep it smart, keep it ethical, and remember—we're here to stop the baddies, not join them.

Email and messaging anonymously

Using an anonymous email address is critical for OSINT investigators who want to obscure their identity and maintain privacy when interacting online. Email addresses often serve as a gateway to a person's real identity, providing clues and links regarding who someone actually is. Without anonymity, the OSINT researcher risks their personal information being exposed if their email is linked to forums, services, or social media used in an investigation. This could make the researcher vulnerable to hacking, doxing, retaliation, or unwanted association with certain groups or causes.

Creating a completely dissociated email address tied to no identifying details is therefore vital for secure, private OSINT work. The anonymous email should never be used for anything that could reveal personal details. It should not be the address listed on social media, professional sites such as LinkedIn, shopping accounts, etc. Ideally, it should be generated using a service such as Proton Mail (`https://protonmail.com/`).

Figure 2.12 – Proton Mail can help to hide your real identity

Alternatively, a Tuta email (`https://tuta.com/`) does not require any valid personal info to create.

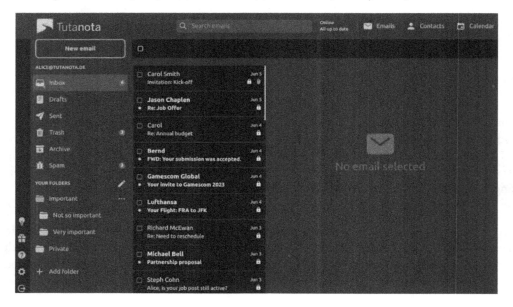

Figure 2.13 – Tutanota anonymous email

Using a dedicated anonymous email address allows the OSINT investigator to register for forums, make inquiries, and communicate without concern that their real identity will be uncovered. It is a critical line of defense to preserve anonymity.

Staying ahead of cyber threats in OSINT

Conducting OSINT investigations comes with inherent cybersecurity risks. With online privacy and anonymity as core principles of ethical OSINT, practitioners must continuously take steps to stay ahead of emerging technological threats. This requires vigilance in keeping up with the latest security issues, learning from past incidents, and improving personal practices.

Keeping up with privacy and security news

Monitoring cybersecurity and privacy news is essential for understanding the ever-evolving risk landscape. Subscribe to threat advisory services such as the following to receive timely notifications on vulnerabilities and new attack methods:

- CIS Cybersecurity Threats (`https://www.cisecurity.org/cybersecurity-threats`)
- US-CERT bulletins (`https://www.cisa.gov/news-events/bulletins`)

One of my personal favorites is in fact the US-CERT bulletins. Not only do they not favor any vendor, but their bulletins are really thorough.

Figure 2.14 – US-CERT bulletins

If you want to be like the cool kids in cyber security, you need to also be reading security blogs and news sites such as these:

- Krebs on Security (https://krebsonsecurity.com/)
- Privacy News Online (https://www.privateinternetaccess.com/blog/)
- SCHMOOZE OSINT (https://www.sangoma.com/)

These resources will help you to stay current on relevant developments.

You should also follow leading information security voices on social media and attend conferences such as DEF CON, Blackhat, or Bsides when possible.

Learning from past breaches and incidents

Studying major past breaches through post-mortem analyses reveals important lessons. The 2016 LinkedIn breach (https://www.forbes.com/sites/daveywinder/2024/01/23/massive-26-billion-record-leak-dropbox-linkedin-twitterx-all-named/?sh=2ab1fc93ab58) exposed how hacked third-party data enabled new attacks through information cascades. High-profile doxing and harassment campaigns such as Gamergate (https://www.nytimes.com/interactive/2019/08/15/opinion/what-is-gamergate.html) spotlight the real-world damages when OSINT is weaponized. Examining practices employed by rogue investigators also explains risks such as social engineering that ethical OSINT researchers must avoid.

Summary

Strong anonymity practices are the OSINT investigator's first line of defense. Routinely search your name online to inventory digital footprints and close any leaks of personal details. Adopt tools such as Tor, virtual phone numbers, and anonymous emails to insulate your real identity. Compartmentalize identifiable information and maintain separate devices and accounts for OSINT activities. Make continuing education on privacy a priority—new identifying threats are always arising.

Ethical OSINT investigators can keep their personal security intact and research safely with vigilance across these areas. The threats are always evolving, so continued effort is required to stay ahead of the game. Up next, we'll look at the methods and techniques that one can use during an OSINT investigation.

The OSINT Toolbox – Methods and Techniques for Gathering and Analyzing Information

Grab yourself a comfy chair and a cup of your favorite brew because you're about to embark on a whirlwind tour through the bustling avenues of **Open Source Intelligence** (**OSINT**). In this chapter, we're unraveling the mysteries and showcasing the sparkle of the OSINT universe, where every nugget of information is a stepping stone toward mastering the art of ethical hacking.

From deciphering the language of the web to donning the hat of a digital detective, we're here to guide you through an adventure that's as exhilarating as a rollercoaster ride through cyberspace. Oh, and don't you worry; we've peppered in a dash of humor to keep that grin on your face as you soak up knowledge.

So, what thrilling stops have we planned on this OSINT adventure, you ask? Here's a sneak peek:

- Introduction to OSINT methods and techniques
- Searching and browsing the surface of the web
- Searching and browsing the surface web
- Delving into the deep and dark web
- Geospatial and imagery analysis
- Automating OSINT collection and analysis

By the end of this chapter, you'll be a maestro adept at gathering and analyzing open source information with finesse and ethical responsibility. You'll have a utility belt brimming with strategies and techniques, ready to take on the OSINT world with gusto.

Introduction to OSINT methods and techniques

In the world of OSINT, there are various techniques and methods available. These tools provide modern investigators with the means to navigate through vast amounts of information effectively. Whether it's exploring lesser-known parts of the internet or using geospatial analysis, the OSINT toolkit is essential for uncovering valuable data. Let's dive into some of these techniques, each vital for ethical hacking and intelligence collection.

So, grab your favorite snack, settle in, and let's saunter through some of these dazzling techniques, each a star in the glittering galaxy of ethical hacking and intelligence gathering. Ready to roll?

The variety of techniques used in OSINT

In the wide and varied domain of OSINT, there exists a plethora of techniques and methods, each offering a distinct pathway to gather and analyze information. These techniques serve as a toolkit for ethical hacking and intelligence gathering. Let's take a closer look at some of these techniques. Ready?

Web scraping

This technique involves programmatically pulling data from websites. It's a cornerstone in the OSINT field, facilitating the rapid and efficient collection of substantial data.

Here are some advantages that web scraping provides to a security researcher:

- **Handy automation**: Think of web scraping like having a tireless digital assistant. This assistant, powered by scripts from languages such as Python, can visit websites and gather the information you need, all while you're sipping your coffee. It's like having a superpower to be everywhere at once, collecting valuable data without breaking a sweat.

- **Gathering the good stuff**: Web scraping is like going on a treasure hunt across the vast ocean of the internet, seeking out the exact pieces of information you need. Whether it's contact information from online directories or juicy tidbits from tech forums, scraping helps you collect these valuable nuggets quickly and efficiently.

- **Keeping a watchful eye**: Web scrapers are like your personal lookouts. They keep an eye on websites for you, alerting you to any changes. This could be super helpful for staying on top of things such as updates or announcements from sites that don't offer handy "*subscribe*" buttons.

- **Time travel through web pages**: Scrapers can act like a time machine for web content. They can take regular snapshots of web pages, allowing you to see what's changed over time. This can be a lifesaver when you need to reference something that's been updated or deleted.

- **Making sense of data**: Once you've got all this data, you can get your detective hat on and look for clues and connections. It's like piecing together a jigsaw puzzle – finding out what all this information means and how it fits into the bigger picture of your OSINT investigation.

- **Supercharging your research**: All the bits and bobs you collect from web scraping can be combined with other data to make your research even more powerful. It's like mixing different colors to get that perfect shade for your painting, enriching the overall picture with more depth and context.

Python, complemented by libraries such as Beautiful Soup, is a popular choice for web scraping endeavors. You can explore it further at `https://www.crummy.com/software/BeautifulSoup/`. This tool assists you in navigating the HTML and XML structures of websites to pinpoint the information you're seeking. Here's a straightforward Python script to initiate you into web scraping with Beautiful Soup:

```
from bs4 import BeautifulSoup
import requests
response = requests.get('https://daledumbsitdown.com')
soup = BeautifulSoup(response.text, 'html.parser')
# Print the page title
print(soup.title.string)
```

Let's break down what this code is trying to do:

1. This step is calling Beautiful Soup into action:

    ```
    from bs4 import BeautifulSoup
    ```

2. Next, we're welcoming the requests, a popular Python library used for making various HTTP requests, such as GET or POST:

    ```
    import requests
    ```

3. Here, we're sending out a GET request to `https://daledumbsitdown.com` to join our exclusive season. The `requests.get()` function fetches the content from the URL, and the content responds to the invitation by being stored in the `response` variable:

    ```
    response = requests.get('https://daledumbsitdown.com')
    ```

4. Now, we're handing over the session to Beautiful Soup. It takes the text content from the response (the session details, if you will) and uses `html.parser` to make sense of the HTML structure, organizing a well-planned event where every tag knows its place:

    ```
    soup = BeautifulSoup(response.text, 'html.parser')
    ```

5. Finally, we're asking Beautiful Soup to create the title of the webpage. Beautiful Soup finds the `<title>` tag in the HTML and prints the text inside it, which is the title of the page:

    ```
    print(soup.title.string)
    ```

So, in essence, this script is your golden ticket to fetching and displaying the title of a webpage. I know this is a simplified example, but it's a solid ground-floor example. As you dig deeper, you'll discover that each technique offers a new layer of complexity and depth, providing a wealth of opportunities to sharpen your skills and broaden your understanding.

Utilizing social media platforms

Platforms such as Twitter, Facebook, LinkedIn, and Instagram are not just entertainment hubs, but they also serve as rich sources of data. I'll dive a little deeper here within this chapter, but for now, let's just talk about why this is a technique. At its core, social media analysis in OSINT revolves around the extraction and analysis of information from various social platforms such as Facebook, Twitter, LinkedIn, and Instagram. The objective is to construct a picture of an organization's personnel and activities, or sometimes to identify potential vulnerabilities.

Here's a list of how professionals might approach this:

- **Profile aggregation**: Security professionals collect and combine data on employees, stakeholders, and the company. They use tools such as Pipl or Spokeo to search for people on various social media platforms, gathering information that can be used to create targeted phishing attacks. This information can include job titles, personal interests, and other relevant details.

- **Content analysis**: Analyzing posts, likes, shares, and comments can uncover patterns of behavior. For instance, an employee discussing or complaining about work-related software on a public forum could inadvertently reveal details about the software stack the company uses.

- **Geolocation and metadata**: Photographs and posts are often tagged with geolocation data. This can unwittingly expose the locations of critical infrastructure, such as server rooms or data centers. Furthermore, the metadata in posted photos can contain the make and model of the device used, potentially giving clues about the organization's issued hardware.

- **Relationship mapping**: Tools such as **Maltego** are employed to visually map relationships between different individuals within the company. By analyzing an individual's network, it's possible to deduce the organizational structure or even discover unofficial connections between employees and other entities, such as suppliers or competitors.

- **Sentiment analysis**: Some security teams go deeper by conducting sentiment analysis on posts to determine morale within a company. Low morale could indicate a higher risk of insider threats or employee negligence, impacting the company's security posture.

- **Event and pattern discovery**: Security analysts look for mentions of system upgrades, patches, or outages that can pinpoint times when an organization's systems may be vulnerable. Likewise, posts about company events can reveal when offices might be empty or when IT staff might be preoccupied with non-security tasks.

- **Recruitment and job postings:** Job listings on LinkedIn or other career sites can reveal technology stacks, ongoing projects, and even future company moves. This is information that can indicate the types of systems in use and potential future expansions or shifts in technology.

Social media OSINT requires a careful balance of respecting privacy while observing from a distance. Analysts typically never interact directly with targets or attempt to infringe on personal privacy settings; instead, they passively collect what is publicly available to inform their security practices.

Understanding the human factor in cybersecurity is the main objective. It's not only about the technology that an organization employs but also about the people who utilize it and discuss it. Thus, social media OSINT is focused on transforming the public footprint of an organization's staff into valuable security intelligence.

Geospatial and imagery analysis

Geospatial analysis is all about diving into geographical data to identify patterns and trends. It's a vital tool in the OSINT toolbox, helping you visualize data in a geographical context, which can often reveal insights that might be missed in a more traditional data analysis. Geospatial analysis is not just about viewing pretty satellite images (although I've been caught in a rabbit hole exploring beyond my objective); it's a powerful tool that can provide valuable insights into various phenomena, from environmental changes to urban development.

First off, let's chat about the wonders of satellite and aerial imagery. These aren't just your average satellite photos that you casually browse on Google Earth. These images can be a treasure trove of data, revealing patterns, movements, and sometimes even undisclosed structures. It's all about harnessing platforms such as Sentinel Hub (https://www.sentinel-hub.com/) to interpret these visuals and extract valuable insights.

Let's shift gears to geolocation techniques, which is where the real fun begins. We're talking about utilizing tools and platforms to pinpoint exact locations, and sometimes even narrowing it down to the exact spot where an image was captured.

As for the cool tools we can use? Search engines such as Google, Bing, and Yandex have map features that can be utilized for an investigation. There are also other tools designed for specific purposes, such as displaying only air traffic or the latest aerial imagery for a region or showing only street cameras:

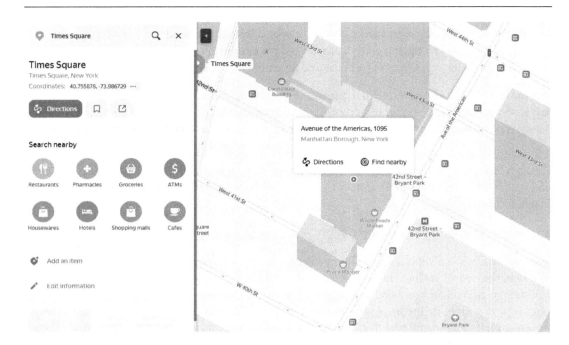

Figure 3.1 – Yandex.com showing a building's coordinates

Law enforcement agencies can employ air and marine traffic tracking tools to monitor criminal activities. Geospatial data sources are rich reservoirs of information for OSINT across various fields.

But we're not stopping there! Image analysis is where we dig even deeper, uncovering clues that might be hidden in plain sight. This involves detailed scrutiny of images, analyzing aspects such as shadows to deduce the time of day an image was taken, or examining backgrounds for signs or landmarks that can offer additional insights. Websites such as FotoForensics (http://fotoforensics.com/) can be a handy tool in this phase, helping you dissect images for hidden information.

Deep and dark web analysis

Deep and dark web analysis involves navigating those hidden corners of the internet to gather information. I know it's spooky when we hear about the dark web, but we'll dive into it a bit deeper later in the book when we look at the tools and techniques required to navigate these parts of the web safely.

Remember, the key to successful OSINT is not only the ability to collect data. It involves using the collected data to make informed decisions and gain a deeper understanding of the target.

Importance of selecting the right method for a specific task

In terms of OSINT, choosing the best technique for a certain assignment is similar to picking the best tool for the job – it may make or break your venture. Let's use a few actual examples to demonstrate this:

- **Corporate espionage prevention**: Imagine you're a cybersecurity consultant tasked with safeguarding a company's trade secrets. Utilizing social media mining techniques could help you monitor employees' online activities to prevent potential leaks. Some of us would call this being a **white hat hacker**.

- **Disaster response**: In the wake of a natural disaster, geospatial analysis can be a lifesaver, *literally*. By analyzing satellite imagery, you can pinpoint affected areas and plan rescue operations more effectively.

- **Market research**: If you want to know how people feel about a product or brand, you can learn a lot by looking at trends and feelings on social media platforms. It's like keeping your finger on the market's pulse!

> Note
>
> In each of these scenarios, selecting the right OSINT method is crucial. It's not just about gathering data but gathering the right data. That reminds me; I don't know if you've ever heard my famous statement when it comes to hacking and in this case OSINT, but here it is in case you haven't: "*Just because you CAN, doesn't mean you CAN.*" So, always adhere to ethical practices when conducting OSINT.

OSINT is a dynamic and versatile field, offering a rich toolbox for those keen on gathering and analyzing open source information. Whether you're web scraping to gather data or mining social media for golden nuggets of information, the right technique can be your key to success.

Searching and browsing the surface web

The surface web, a vast repository of information indexed by search engines, is a critical resource in OSINT. Let me try to equip you with the skills and knowledge to effectively navigate the surface web, utilizing a range of techniques to gather valuable data.

Advanced search engine techniques

Search engines are my go-to allies in navigating the surface web. However, to truly unlock their potential, it's essential to master the art of advanced search techniques. These techniques empower you to fine-tune your searches, pinpointing the exact piece of information you're after.

For example, leveraging operators such as `site:` to sift through a specific website or `intext:` to locate web pages containing a certain phrase can be game changers. These refined techniques streamline your search process, helping you zero in on the most relevant results without wading through a sea of unrelated content.

One of my favorites is the `site:` operator; this bad boy allows you to search a specific website. How can this help? Well, it's really useful when you are looking for detailed information from a known source. Here's a breakdown of how it works:

```
site:daledumbsitdown.com "cyber security"
```

In this query, the search results will only display pages from `daledumbsitdown.com` that contain the phrase `cyber security`. Easy, huh?

The `intext:` operator, on the other hand, helps you find web pages containing a particular phrase. It will streamline your search process. Check this out:

```
intext:"recent cyber attacks"
```

This query will return web pages that contain the exact phrase `recent cyber attacks`, helping you find recent information on cyber attacks quickly. I know, right?!

Mastering the combination of different operators can further enhance your search capabilities, enabling you to locate highly specific information swiftly. This skill is invaluable in OSINT, where precise and quick data retrieval is often necessary.

Google hacking

Google hacking, or **Google dorking**, is a technique that leverages advanced search operators to find specific information or possible vulnerabilities on websites indexed by Google. This technique is a cornerstone in OSINT, enabling researchers to locate sensitive data or data leaks that might be publicly accessible on the internet.

For instance, the `filetype:` operator can be used to find documents of a specific type on a particular topic. Try going to Google and typing in the following:

```
filetype:pdf "annual security report
```

This query will return PDF documents that contain the phrase `annual security report`, potentially providing detailed insights into security trends and incidents. Now put on your evil hat for a second and think about what hackers might be searching for about your organization.

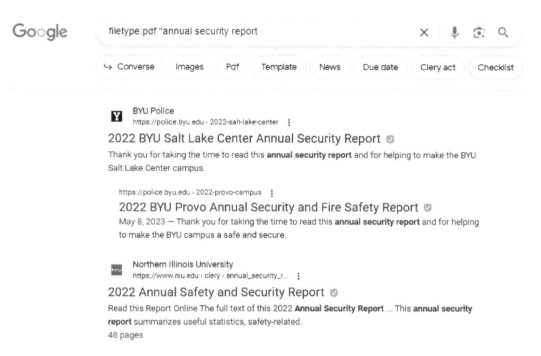

Figure 3.2 – Using "filetype:pdf "annual security report" shows interesting data

Scared yet? No? Then check this out.

The `inurl:` operator can help find URLs containing a specific keyword, sometimes leading to exposed directories or sensitive information. Here's how it can be used:

```
inurl:admin login
```

This query will return URLs that contain the words `admin` and `login`, which might sometimes lead to some really interesting websites. Go ahead, try it; I'll wait.

As you become more comfortable with basic operators, you can start to combine them to create more complex queries. This could help you uncover a wealth of information that might not be easily accessible through regular search methods. Here are some advanced techniques and examples:

```
intext:"Login" inurl:/secure
```

This query combines two Google search operators: `intext:` and `inurl:`. Here's what each part of the query does:

- `intext:"Login"`: The `intext:` operator is used to search for a specific word or phrase within the content of web pages. In this case, it is looking for web pages that contain the word `Login` in the text of the page. This could potentially return pages where there is a login form.

- `inurl:/secure`: The `inurl:` operator searches for a specific word or phrase in the URL of web pages. Here, it is looking for URLs that contain the word `/secure`. This might indicate that the page is a secure section of the website, possibly a login or admin page.

So, this combination might be used to find secure login pages of websites. It's a query that could potentially be used to find pages with security vulnerabilities, as it might return pages where sensitive data or functionalities are housed.

How about this one (I know, I'm getting all Google dorkin' on you):

```
intitle:"index of" ".ssh" OR "ssh_config" OR "ssh_known_hosts" OR
"authorized_keys" OR "id_rsa" OR "id_dsa"
```

Can you guess? I'll give you a second; there are several operators here. Ready?

When combined, this query looks for directory listings (indicated by `index of` in the title) that contain any of the specified **Secure Shell** (**SSH**) configurations or key files. Let me break it down further:

- `intitle:"index of"`: The `intitle:` operator searches for pages with specific words or phrases in the title. Here it's looking for pages with the title `"index of"`. This title is commonly found in directory listings on web servers, where the results of directories are visible as web pages.

- `".ssh" OR "ssh_config" OR "ssh_known_hosts" OR "authorized_keys" OR "id_rsa" OR "id_dsa"`: This part of the query is looking for pages that contain several terms. Each of these terms is associated with SSH configuration and key files, which are used to authenticate and secure connections to servers. Let me break them down a bit more for you:

  - `.ssh`: This would be a directory that typically contains an SSH configuration and key files.

  - `ssh_config`: A file that contains client-side SSH configuration settings.

  - `ssh_known_hosts`: A file that stores host keys, helping the SSH client validate their identities to the servers.

  - `authorized_keys`: Contains public keys for SSH authentication, allowing users with the corresponding private keys to log in.

  - `id_rsa`: This file contains a user's RSA private key for SSH authentication.

  - `id_dsa`: A file that contains a user's DSA private key, and it's used in SSH authentication.

  - The OR operator is used to search for pages that contain any one of the listed terms, meaning that the search will return pages that contain any of the filenames or directory names specified in the query.

Personally, I could write a whole book on Google hacking/dorking. This is another tool that could lead you down so many rabbit holes such as finding security cameras, **Internet of Things (IoT)** devices, SharePoint login pages, and even printers. Yeah, there's nothing like sending some company's printer a print job of *War and Peace* to prove the point that they are exposed.

Utilizing specialized search engines and directories

Specialized search engines and directories are foundational resources for researchers, especially in the OSINT field. These tools are designed to focus on specific areas, offering better and more unique information than you might find on mainstream search engines. In this section, we will navigate through the various facets of these platforms and how they can be effectively utilized in OSINT.

Specialized search engines are platforms that concentrate on a particular type of information, offering a more targeted approach to data gathering. These engines are designed to provide in-depth information in their respective fields. Here, we will explore different categories of specialized search engines and their utilities in OSINT.

Academic search engines

Think of academic search engines as your secret pass to the exclusive library of cyber wisdom, where a simple search can unlock a world of scholarly gossip that could totally level up your OSINT game:

- **Google Scholar** (`scholar.google.com`): Google Scholar is like the VIP lounge of the internet where all the scholarly articles, theses, books, conference papers, and patents come to mingle. You'll actually find some of the most well-researched papers without wading through the riff-raff you might encounter on the regular Google.

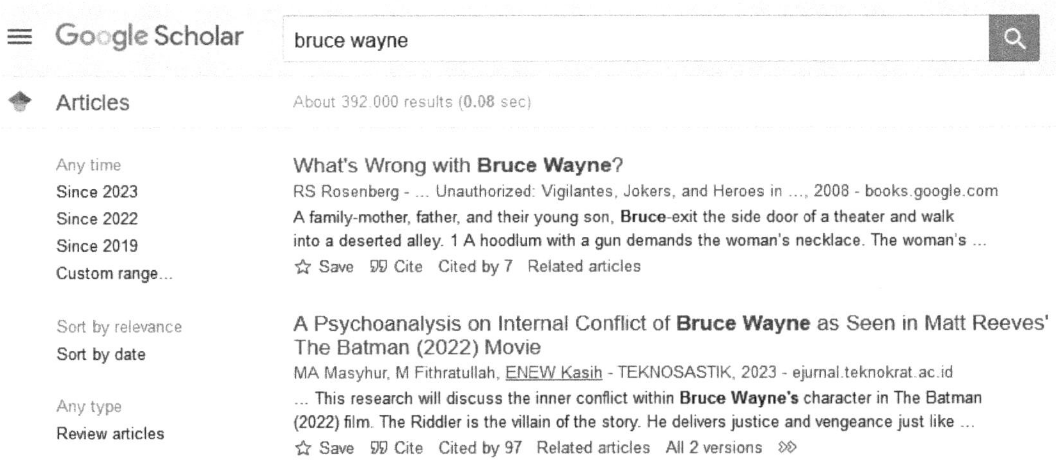

Figure 3.3 – Results for Bruce Wayne on scholar.google.com

- **PubMed** (`pubmed.ncbi.nlm.nih.gov`): Meet PubMed, your go-to buddy for all things biomedical and life sciences. It's on a mission to boost health levels worldwide, and yes, that includes your personal well being, too!

  Now, let's talk numbers – this database is brimming with over 36 million citations and abstracts, making it a valuable collection of biomedical literature. While it might not hand over full-text journal articles on a silver platter, it's got your back with handy links to the full texts, whenever available. So, whether it's from the publisher's website or the ever-reliable **PubMed Central** (**PMC**), you're just a click away from diving deep into the world of science.

- **IEEE Xplore** (`https://ieeexplore.ieee.org/Xplore/home.jsp`): This is a digital library offering comprehensive access to professional literature in electrical engineering, computer science, and electronics, known for its high-quality content. It is a valuable resource for tech enthusiasts looking for in-depth studies and papers.

Code search engines

These platforms not only host countless open source projects but occasionally become inadvertent sources of sensitive data and insights into software vulnerabilities:

- **GitHub** (`github.com`): Ah, GitHub. This site/search engine is where developers store their projects. It really is a little goldmine for finding open source projects and code snippets, and it sometimes even reveals sensitive information or security vulnerabilities in software projects.

- **SourceForge** (`sourceforge.net`): This is another great site/search engine. SourceForge allows users to find, create, and publish open source software for free. Here, you can find a wide variety of software projects as well as team up with other developers.

Patent search engines

Here's where you can explore cutting-edge innovation and the blueprints of inventions that shape our world:

- **Google Patents** (`patents.google.com`): This offers detailed insights into patents, providing a deep understanding of technological advancements and market competition.

- **United States Patent and Trademark Office (USPTO) Database** (`uspto.gov`): The *"big boy"* of patents. It provides detailed information on various patents, including descriptions, claims, and citations, offering a deep insight into the world of inventions and innovations.

Image search engines

Visual search engines can play a pivotal role in pinpointing security vulnerabilities and potential threats by displaying images of system infrastructures, web applications, networks, and even passwords scribbled on sticky notes, as seen in this TV interview from TV5Monde back in 2015:

Figure 3.4 – A TV interview with passwords on sticky notes in the background

Whether it's verifying the authenticity of images or uncovering associated information, these tools are key:

- **TinEye** (`tineye.com`): This is a cool reverse image search engine that allows users to find the origin of an image or locate other instances of its use online. I use this tool all the time to help me in OSINT, for verifying the authenticity of images or finding information related to a specific image.

- **Google Images** (`images.google.com`): This stands as a favored choice among search platforms owing to its user friendliness and extensive repository of visuals. It operates on Google's vast database, which could potentially serve as a goldmine for identifying vulnerable points for cyberattacks. Individuals with malicious intent might utilize image and video search platforms to monitor network activities in real time, providing them with current insights into the evolving nature of their targets. This timely access to data enables them to swiftly detect alterations in a system or network, allowing them to strategize and respond accordingly.

Alright, so we've had our fun rummaging through image search engines, right? It's pretty wild what you can dig up with just a few clicks. But hey, that's just part of the story. Now, let's switch gears and talk about the social media jungle. It's where the action's at—constantly updating and buzzing with new info. Think of it as the difference between catching a rerun and watching the live show. On social media, we're getting the play-by-play on people and companies, and let me tell you, it's a gold mine for OSINT work. So, let's jump in and see what fresh intel we can gather from the social feeds.

Exploring social media for OSINT (SOCMINT)

SOCMINT, the more nuanced sibling of OSINT, has particular expertise in unearthing information from the bustling world of social media platforms. While OSINT is quite content to peruse publicly available data, SOCMINT isn't afraid to venture a bit further, potentially accessing information that was initially shared within more closed circles on social media platforms.

Social media platforms have transformed into bustling hubs of information where individuals and organizations share updates, opinions, and news. These platforms have become essential tools in the OSINT toolkit, offering a ton of data that can be analyzed for many purposes. Let's delve into some popular social media platforms and how they can be utilized as OSINT goldmines:

- **X (formerly Twitter)** (`twitter.com`):

  - **The buzz station**: Twitter is pretty much the hotspot for all the latest gossip and breaking news. It's where OSINT analysts hang out to grab the newest scoops on just about everything currently happening.

  - **Search, but with style**: Twitter's got this cool search feature that lets you sift through tweets with all kinds of filters, making it a piece of cake for OSINT analysts to nail down the exact information they're after.

  - **API coolness**: Oh, and Twitter's API integration is a real time saver, helping researchers to gather a whole bunch of data without breaking a sweat.

- **Facebook** (`facebook.com`):

  - **Chat rooms galore**: Facebook is this giant hangout spot with a ton of communities and forums where people share information on a wide array of topics. It's a goldmine for OSINT analysts looking to dig up some fresh data.

  - **Marketplace hustle**: The Facebook Marketplace is buzzing with activity, with folks buying and selling stuff left and right. It's a great place for analysts to catch up on the latest market trends and consumer behaviors.

  - **Event buzz**: Then there's Facebook Events, a handy tool for creating and promoting events. It's a neat feature for researchers to gather some intel on different events and the crowd that's attending.

- **LinkedIn** (`linkedin.com`):

  - **Networking hub**: LinkedIn is basically the hub for professional connections, offering a treasure chest of information on companies, industries, and the movers and shakers in the business world, making it a hotspot for business research.

  - **Job board**: It's also the place to check out job postings and get a peek into what's happening in the job market and industry trends.

> **Note**
>
> Job boards are my happy place, as I can gather so much intel on a target just from their job listings.

- **Content central**: LinkedIn users are always sharing a bunch of stuff, from articles to presentations, making it a rich source of information for OSINT researchers to dive into.

- **Instagram** (`instagram.com`):

  - **Visual wonderland**: Instagram is all about visuals, offering a sea of images and videos that are perfect for different kinds of analyses, from spotting trends to analyzing sentiments.

  - **Tagging magic**: Instagram has cool features such as hashtags and geotags that help users categorize and find content, making it a handy tool for OSINT researchers to track down specific information.

  - **Influencer watch**: Instagram is also home to a bunch of influencers who have a big say in shaping opinions. Keeping an eye on their content and strategies can give you a peek into social media trends and what the public is thinking.

OK, now that we know the intel type we're dealing with, let's see what we can do with it.

SOCMINT concepts – a deep dive

It's essential to grasp the various concepts and terminologies that form the backbone of SOCMINT. Let's dig in here:

- **Details about a user's profile**: This static data provides a brief overview of the identity a user presents online, either personally or professionally. A user's LinkedIn page might include information about their current job as a "Windows Admin," as well as their educational background and skill sets such as "Exchange 2013" or "SharePoint." User's hobbies and the kind of information they typically engage with may be displayed on their Twitter profile, providing insight into their personality and preferences.

- **Interactions**: This aspect covers the dynamic activities users engage in on social media platforms. For example, on Facebook, a user might be actively participating in a group discussion about the latest developments in cybersecurity, sharing insights or resources. On platforms such as Instagram, interactions could involve commenting on a post about wireless security tools or sharing a story that highlights a recent webinar on ethical hacking. These interactions are a goldmine of data, offering a real-time view of users' opinions, discussions, and the content they resonate with.

- **Metadata**: This refers to the contextual data that accompanies the primary content shared on social media platforms. For instance, a photo that has been posted might have all kinds of metadata goodies, such as the geographical location, the time and date of the post, and the type of device used for the upload. This metadata can offer deeper insights into users' behaviors and patterns, helping researchers to build a more comprehensive profile of individuals or groups.

> **Note**
>
> The information that folks don't understand they're exposing on social media sites is staggering. Some people expose everything from their name, gender, email addresses, and kids' names. But the really scary thing for me is when people post photos of their kids online. Why? Well, rule number 1 is once it's on the internet you *cannot* take it back. Rule 2, parents have a tendency to list their children's names. Photos often contain information you didn't recognize as being something that might put them in danger, such as a photo of their first day of school in front of their house, which might have the house address on it. OK, I'm getting off my security soapbox.

There are two types of data in this world

Technically, there are two different types of data that you'll find:

- **Explicit information**: This is the kind of data that users willingly share on their social media platforms. It's the straightforward, no-beating-around-the-bush kind of information that forms the visible layer of a user's online persona. For instance, a user might openly share their views on the latest developments in the cybersecurity world in a Tweet, or post a LinkedIn update about a recent certification they've achieved in ethical hacking. This category also includes profile details such as job titles, educational backgrounds, and the groups or communities they are part of. Explicit information serves as a direct window into a user's professional life, interests, and opinions, offering a clear-cut view of their online activities and engagements.

- **Implicit information**: This is the more subtle, often unintentional, data that users reveal online. Let me give you an example: by analyzing the patterns of a user's likes and shares on platforms such as Facebook, researchers might be able to deduce their preferences, affiliations, or inclinations toward certain topics or communities. Similarly, the metadata attached to the content they share, such as location tags or device types, can offer clues about their habits, locations they frequent, or the kind of devices they use. Implicit information, therefore, serves as a rich reservoir of insights that can help researchers build a more nuanced and comprehensive profile of individuals, often revealing patterns and details that are not immediately apparent.

By harnessing both explicit and implicit information, SOCMINT researchers can weave together a detailed tapestry of insights, helping them to conduct more rounded and insightful investigations. It's like putting together the pieces of a puzzle, where each piece, whether explicit or implicit, adds a new dimension to the overall picture.

You need to "Sherlock it"

This is a phrase my kids are sick of. Whenever they ask me a question that I think they should be able to use common sense to figure out the answer to, I say "*Sherlock it.*" Imagine how happy I was when this tool came out!

Sherlock is this handy-dandy tool that helps you hunt down a person's or organization's username across a bunch of social media platforms. It's like your personal detective that lets you pop in a name or username and then scours the internet to find any social media profiles that might be linked to that name or username.

Let's give it a whirl. These are the instructions to install it on a Kali box, which is my go-to system for OSINT:

1. **Update your system**: Before we invite Sherlock into our digital abode, let's make sure everything is spick and span. Open your terminal and run the following command to update your system:

   ```
   sudo apt update && sudo apt upgrade -y
   ```

2. **Install Git**: Now, we need to ensure that Git, the popular version control system, is installed on your Kali system. It's like the digital toolbox for our Sherlock installation. Run this command to install Git:

   ```
   sudo apt install git -y
   ```

   This command politely asks your system to install Git and automatically agrees to the terms and conditions (hence, -y).

3. **Clone Sherlock repository**: Next, we're going to clone the Sherlock repository from GitHub. It's like Sherlock's home where he keeps all his detective tools. Use this command to clone the repository:

   ```
   git clone https://github.com/sherlock-project/sherlock.git
   ```

4. **Install requirements**: Before we can start using Sherlock, we need to set up the environment properly. Move into the Sherlock directory and run this command to install the requirements:

   ```
   python3 -m pip install -r requirements.txt
   ```

5. Now that Sherlock is installed, let's give it a whirl. Just use this simple command:

   ```
   sherlock <username>
   ```

Now, keep in mind that the results might be a hit or miss. For a little sneak peek, here's a screenshot of a search for the username `dalemeredith`:

```
┌──(kali㉿kali)-[~]
└─$ sherlock dalemeredith
[*] Checking username dalemeredith on:

[+] About.me: https://about.me/dalemeredith
[+] Audiojungle: https://audiojungle.net/user/dalemeredith
[+] Behance: https://www.behance.net/dalemeredith
[+] Disqus: https://disqus.com/dalemeredith
[+] Facebook: https://www.facebook.com/dalemeredith
[+] Fiverr: https://www.fiverr.com/dalemeredith
[+] Flipboard: https://flipboard.com/@dalemeredith
[+] GeeksforGeeks: https://auth.geeksforgeeks.org/user/dalemeredith
[+] Gravatar: http://en.gravatar.com/dalemeredith
[+] Houzz: https://houzz.com/user/dalemeredith
[+] Instagram: https://www.instagram.com/dalemeredith
[+] Issuu: https://issuu.com/dalemeredith
[+] NationStates Nation: https://nationstates.net/nation=dalemeredith
[+] NationStates Region: https://nationstates.net/region=dalemeredith
[+] Periscope: https://www.periscope.tv/dalemeredith/
[+] Reddit: https://www.reddit.com/user/dalemeredith
[+] SlideShare: https://slideshare.net/dalemeredith
[+] Smule: https://www.smule.com/dalemeredith
[+] Snapchat: https://www.snapchat.com/add/dalemeredith
[+] Strava: https://www.strava.com/athletes/dalemeredith
[+] ThemeForest: https://themeforest.net/user/dalemeredith
[+] TrashboxRU: https://trashbox.ru/users/dalemeredith
```

Figure 3.5 – Using Sherlock against the username dalemeredith

Whether you're on the hunt for clues about a username or just trying to connect the online dots, Sherlock's your go-to buddy. It's straightforward, no-nonsense, and, honestly, a bit of a game changer for anyone in the cyber-sleuthing biz.

Hashtags and geolocations

When it comes to digging up some golden nuggets of information online, using hashtags and geolocation can be your best pals. It's like having a secret map that leads you straight to the treasure of data you're after.

These little guys, marked by the # symbol, are like the breadcrumbs that lead you to the heart of buzzing conversations and trending topics. Picture this: you're keen on keeping tabs on the latest chatter about, oh, I don't know, how about the coolest hero ever. Let's pick someone with no superpowers, someone who runs around at night in a cape. I know; let's say Batman. Just pop into your favorite social media platform and search #Batman, and bam! You're now in the epicenter of all the latest discussions and insights. It's a fantastic way to stay in the loop and gather real-time intel. Here's how to wield hashtags effectively:

- **Trend analysis**: Tools such as **Hashtagify** (https://hashtagify.me/) and **RiteTag** (https://ritetag.com/) can be your guiding stars in the hashtag universe. They help you pinpoint trending hashtags and even suggest the optimal ones to amplify your reach. It's like having a backstage pass to the hottest topics creating waves online.

- **Community engagement**: Platforms such as **TweetDeck** (`https://tweetdeck.twitter.com/`) can be your command center for monitoring and engaging with communities revolving around specific hashtags. It's your gateway to immerse yourself in niche discussions and gather firsthand insights from the epicenter of the conversation.

- **Content Discovery: BuzzSumo** (`https://buzzsumo.com/`) is your trusty companion in the quest for discovering popular content based on hashtags. It's your magnifying glass to zoom in on the content that's garnering attention in your field of interest.

Then we have geolocations

A geolocation is the digital equivalent of saying, "*X marks the spot!*" You can pinpoint the geographical coordinates (latitude and longitude) of any device connected to the internet. Any device: your phone, tablet, or even your nifty watch. This fascinating technology branches into three main types: server-based, device-based, and combined data collection:

- **Server-based data collection: The IP sleuth**

  This approach is akin to having a digital sleuth that traces the physical locations linked to IP addresses, thanks to years of data mining. However, the accuracy is as good as the data provided by third-party service providers, sometimes making the data integrity a bit of a guessing game. It's like having a map with ever-changing landmarks where the service providers dictate the standards and offer customized geolocation solutions.

- **Device-based data collection: The GPS whisperer**

  This method is like having a mini detective in your pocket, constantly whispering the whereabouts of your device. It primarily relies on GPS and cellular networks, offering more accuracy in densely populated areas. However, in less-populated regions, it might get a bit *directionally challenged*, leading to data delays or gaps. It's essential to enable location detection on each device and app to make the most of this method but remember that it's always a good idea to keep an eye on privacy concerns.

- **Combined data collection: The best of both worlds**

  This method is like having a dynamic duo of detectives, combining device-based and server-based detection strengths to offer a more comprehensive insight. It ensures a better user experience by providing a fallback option if one data collection method fails, making it a reliable choice for websites aiming to enhance visitor interaction.

- **Geolocation tracking in the real world**

  Google was actively working with law enforcement organizations to support the investigations into the incidents that occurred in the United States on January 6, 2021. Geofencing warrants, which allow the authorities to ask for information on devices that were in a specified location at a particular time, make this collaboration easier. Although this technique has been successful in locating suspects, it has also raised concerns about privacy because it may also collect information on innocent people. Google is negotiating this tricky situation in an attempt to strike a balance between aiding in the investigations and protecting user privacy.

This incident highlights the crucial part that tech firms can play in advancing criminal investigations in the current digital era. The delicate balance between assisting law enforcement and protecting user privacy is also highlighted. Keeping this balance is essential for maintaining public trust and cooperation. A harmonic balance must be achieved as technology develops in order to guarantee that justice is done without jeopardizing people's privacy. This indicates to me a future where technology and law enforcement may combine more regularly, but with required safeguards in place to preserve individual rights; at least, that's my hope. I'm still scared anytime I see any government getting involved with technology.

The magical world of EXIF data

The **EXIF data** in a photo is really the star of the show. This tiny genius stealthily infuses itself into the photos you take with your phone or digital camera, storing a wealth of data such as its GPS coordinates that may be used to retrace your steps to the precise spot where the shot was taken. This must be a breeze, right? Nevertheless, here's the catch: in order to safeguard users' privacy, most websites and social media sites eliminate this information. Hence, a complete EXIF image is as rare as a needle in a haystack while searching the internet. You're in for a real treat, though, if you can track down the original artwork. That being said, you can use tools such as **Jimpl** (`Jimpl.com`) to extract EXIF of a photo. Here, let me upload one for you:

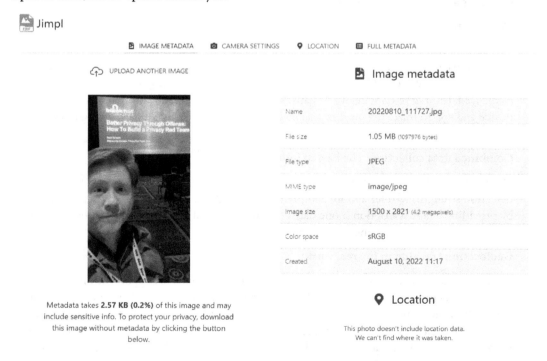

Figure 3.6 – Jimpl.com looking at my photo information

Now, you'll notice that my location's information wasn't available; this is because I've turned location tracking off for my photos as well as for this particular photo, which was taken at Blackhat, and my phone is locked down pretty tight. But look at the metadata that it did pull:

📷 Camera settings

Make	samsung
Model	SM-S908U
Focal length	3.8 mm
Aperture	2.2
Exposure	1/20
ISO	1000
Flash	No Flash

Figure 3.7 – Jumpi even detected my camera settings

ExifTool is a popular program used by those who need to look into or edit the metadata of multimedia files. Now, ExifTool is built into Kali, so let's fire up our Kali systems and see what it can do.

Your first step into the world of metadata manipulation is learning how to read the existing metadata in a file. You can do this by using a simple command:

```
exiftool yourmasterpiece.jpg
```

This command will reveal all the metadata secrets that yourmasterpiece.jpg holds, including details such as the camera settings used and the date it was created.

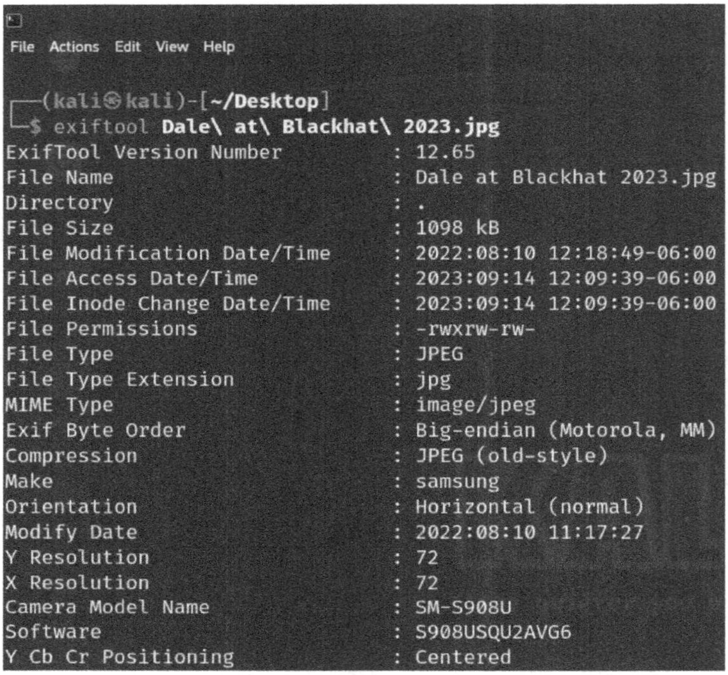

Figure 3.8 – Results from ExifTool on the photo "Dale at Blackhat 2023.jpg"

As you grow more comfortable with ExifTool, you'll discover it has a plethora of advanced features waiting to be explored. From handling multiple files at once to copying metadata between files, the possibilities are vast. Dive into the documentation or use the -h option to uncover more functionalities.

Understanding hidden sources

First off, it's vital to comprehend what **hidden sources** entail. These could be obscure forums, websites, or databases that remain unindexed by mainstream search engines, which makes them a bit elusive. Then there's the data that's in plain sight but often ignored, such as devices that are exposed to the internet with little or no security. These niches might house invaluable data that offer insights or intelligence unavailable on the surface web.

Diving into the deep and dark web

Hold on tight, because we're going to be exploring the deep and dark web, two regions of the internet that have seen relatively little exploration. For the most part, the deep web is content that isn't accessible through traditional search engines. It's not all underhanded dealings; most of it involves databases, sensitive information, and paid memberships. OK, there are a lot of underhanded things going on here too, but let's not focus on that.

Let's make sure we understand the internet

First things first, I need to make sure you understand that the internet itself has *layers*. Yep, the internet is more than just you and Google Chrome typing in www.daledumbsitdown.com to read up on some technology stuff, or going shopping on Amazon.

Now, the internet is like an iceberg. What we usually surf is just the tip, the part visible above the water. The deep web and the dark web, however, are the massive parts underneath, hidden from plain sight. It's where the internet keeps its secrets, its ancient scrolls, if you will.

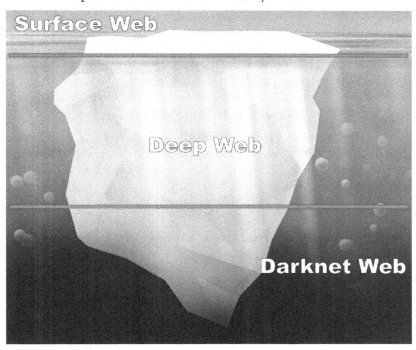

Figure 3.9 – The layers of the internet: surface web, deep web, and darknet web

But fear not, because I'm here to be your torchbearer as we venture into this unknown territory.

- **Layer 1: The surface web**

  Imagine we're just dipping our toes into the ocean. Here, we find the surface web – the shiny, bustling metropolis of the internet. Picture websites such as YouTube, Wikipedia, and basically anything you can access through a straightforward Google search. You could think of this layer as the *public square* of the internet – easily accessible, bustling with activity, and fully indexed by traditional search engines.

- **Layer 2: The deep web**

  As we put on our diving gear to explore further, we stumble upon the deep web, where things get a little mysterious. This section of the internet is like an enormous library archive. It contains databases, personal email accounts, subscription services, and confidential data. It's much larger than the surface web and isn't indexed by regular search engines. Imagine having a VIP pass to a secret club where access is only granted to those in the know – that's what venturing into the deep web is like!

- **Layer 3: The darknet web**

  Here we go, we're about to dive even deeper, into the most secluded corners of the internet – the dark web. Picture a labyrinthine market hidden in the recesses of the city, where every alley holds a secret. It's a small portion of the deep web that has been intentionally hidden and is inaccessible through web browsers. Here, anonymity is the name of the game, with users primarily utilizing browsers such as Tor to mask their identities and activities. But remember, with great power comes great responsibility; this layer can be a hub for illicit activities, so it's essential to tread with caution and ethics at the forefront.

When it comes to OSINT, the surface web is essentially your starting line, a space teeming with accessible information ready to be tapped into. It's the portion of the internet that's indexed by search engines, making it a straightforward access point for anyone with a knack for online exploration. Let's dive into how you can maneuver through this space effectively to gather a wealth of data:

1. **Get Yourself a VPN**

   First things first, get yourself a **Virtual Private Network** (**VPN**) to hide your online activity. This helpful app will hide your IP address, protecting your privacy online.

2. **Download a browser**

   Next up is downloading a browser that will work on the dark web. These include Tor Browser, Waterfox, and Freenet to name a few. These browsers allow you to access websites with the `.onion` domain, which are exclusive to the dark web.

3. **Start your journey with a search engine**

   Now that you're all set up, it's time to start exploring! But wait, Google won't be of any help here. You'll need to use a search engine that specializes in finding `.onion` websites. A popular choice is DuckDuckGo, which you can access at `https://duckduckgo.com/`. It's your trusty guide in this uncharted territory.

4. **Explore .onion Websites**

   With your browser ready and your search engine at hand, you're all set to explore `.onion` websites. But tread carefully, as not all corners of the dark web are safe. Stick to known websites and avoid any shady-looking links. It's a wild west out there, so keep your wits about you!

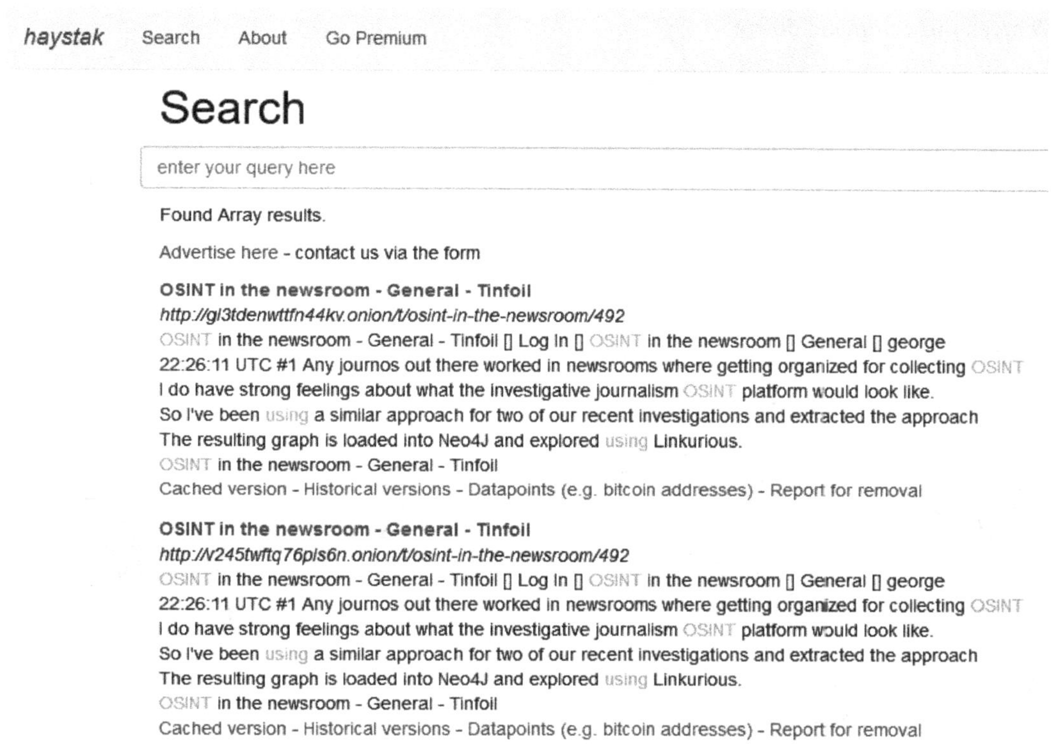

Figure 3.10 – Using Tor and searching for OSINT on haystak's search engine (notice the .onion domain)

As you venture deeper, remember to always prioritize your safety. Keep in mind that this is not a trip for the faint of heart, but with the proper safeguards and equipment, you can safely and securely explore the depths of the internet.

Harvesting more with theHarvester

theHarvester, which is included in Kali, is a program that collects email addresses, subdomains, hostnames, and employee names from a variety of sources, such as search engines, PGP key servers, and the deep web. It is commonly used by security professionals and researchers during the early stages of a penetration test or cyber investigation for information gathering and reconnaissance. To run theHarvester, open a terminal and use the following syntax:

```
theHarvester -d <domain> -l <limit>-b <source>
```

Let's break this command down:

- -d: This specifies the domain you want to search for.

- -l: This limits the number of results.

- -b: This specifies the search source you want to use. Google, Bing, PGP, LinkedIn, and Twitter are all possible values. It's worth noting that you'll need to go into some of these sources and install API keys; if you don't, you'll get errors for those specific sources.

So, let's do this for real:

```
theHarvester -d hackthissite.org -l 500 -b all
```

The output is shown in the following screenshot:

```
[*] Interesting Urls found: 13
------------------------------
http://mail-old.hackthissite.org
https://hackthissite.org/
https://mail.hackthissite.org/
https://mail.hackthissite.org/?r=/login
https://stats.hackthissite.org/
https://www.hackthissite.org/
https://www.hackthissite.org/?adlt=strict
https://www.hackthissite.org/missions/
https://www.hackthissite.org/missions/basic/11/
https://www.hackthissite.org/missions/basic/11/e/l/t/o/n/
https://www.hackthissite.org/missions/realistic/12/cgi-bin/internet.pl
https://www.hackthissite.org/missions/realistic/2/
https://www.hackthissite.org/missions/realistic/9/

[*] LinkedIn Links found: 0
------------------------------

[*] IPs found: 45
------------------------------
67.21.66.227
67.21.66.228
67.21.66.229
67.21.66.230
89.41.169.49
89.106.200.1
137.74.187.100
137.74.187.101
```

Figure 3.11 – Results from theHarvester

Now, the output I got back was way more than I could include in a screenshot. Let's just say it was a plethora of data.

Shodan

Shodan (https://shodan.io) is like Google for IoT. Shodan can help you find and connect to all sorts of devices and services that are connected to the internet. While most folks will use Shodan to check whether their webcam has been hacked, security professionals have a different use in mind. We search Shodan for flaws in a wide range of internet-connected equipment, from web servers to industrial control systems.

We can find a ton of juicy targets using Shodan, and even better, we can do it all from the comfort of our own laptop.

You can begin by simply typing the domain name you want to scan into the web interface:

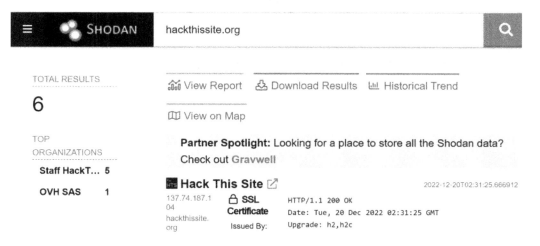

Figure 3.12 – Using Shodan.io to search hackthissite.org

Most of the results for hackthissite.org are about SSL certificates, but if they have IoT devices such as cameras or certain sensors, remote desktop software, or systems as a whole that are exposed to the internet and aren't set up correctly, they will show up here. Here's a suggestion: type os:windows 7 into the search box to ask Shodan to show you any Windows 7 systems it can find:

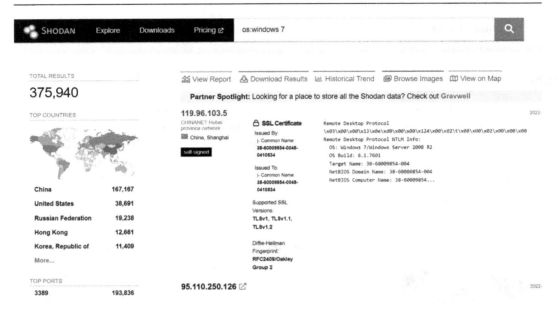

Figure 3.13 – Looks like we can still see over 375,000 Windows 7 systems online

It's surprising to see that there are 375,940 systems running Windows 7 in 2023. Wow, talk about potential targets for security breaches.

One feature of Shodan is the ability to monitor sites/IP addresses for any new devices that might get installed. Shodan's monitoring features allow cybersecurity professionals to observe and track activities within a specified IP range, in this case, 71.6.146.0/24. This is crucial for several reasons:

- **Detecting new devices**: By monitoring this range, you can identify when new devices are connected to the network. This is vital to ensure that only authorized devices are present and to detect potential unauthorized or rogue devices that may pose a security threat.

- **Identifying vulnerabilities**: Shodan can provide information about known vulnerabilities associated with the devices in the specified IP range. This enables you to proactively address these vulnerabilities before they are exploited.

- **Tracking changes and anomalies**: Monitoring allows for the observation of changes in the network configuration or behavior. This includes changes in open ports, services running on the devices, or updates in firmware versions. Anomalies in these areas can be indicators of a security incident.

- **Historical data analysis**: Shodan stores historical data, which can be useful for analyzing trends over time within the IP range. This can help in understanding the evolution of the network's security posture.

- **Alerting on specific criteria**: You can set up alerts in Shodan to be notified when certain conditions are met within the IP range. For example, alerts can be configured for when a new device appears, or a new service is detected.

To effectively use Shodan for monitoring 71.6.146.0/24, you would typically follow these steps:

1. **Set up monitoring**: Configure Shodan to monitor the IP range 71.6.146.0/24. This involves specifying the range in your monitoring settings.

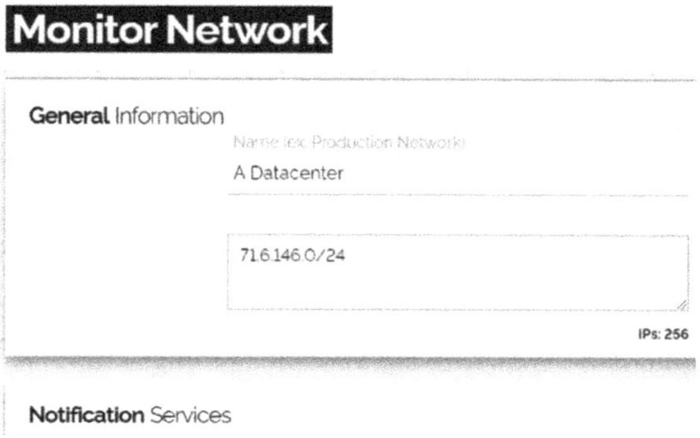

Monitor Network

General Information

Name (ex: Production Network)

A Datacenter

71.6.146.0/24

IPs: 256

Notification Services

Figure 3.14 – Shodan's monitoring feature is powerful for tracking changes

2. **Define alerts**: Based on your security needs, define the criteria for alerts. This could be the appearance of new devices, the exposure of vulnerable services, or unexpected changes in device configurations.

3. **Regularly review reports**: Shodan provides reports based on the monitoring. Regular review of these reports is essential to stay updated on the network status and to spot potential security issues.

Figure 3.15 – Shodan exposes services, ports, and vulnerabilities

4. **Respond to alerts**: When an alert is triggered, it should be investigated to determine whether it represents a genuine security threat or a benign change.

By effectively utilizing the monitoring features of Shodan, you can maintain a strong awareness of the security state of the network within the specified IP range, enabling a proactive stance against potential cybersecurity threats.

Automating OSINT collection and analysis

Alright, let's chat about how AI is shaking things up within OSINT. It's like giving a supercharger to your data-gathering and analysis engine, making everything faster, smarter, and, let's face it, it's just plain cooler.

So, where could AI come into play? Well, here are a couple of things I think AI will step up:

- **Web scraping**: It's this nifty trick where AI helps you pull out heaps of data from various online spots such as news sites and social forums.

- **Sentiment analysis**: This is basically the art of figuring out the vibe around a specific topic by sifting through tons of text data.

- **Image recognition**: AI has got this covered too, pulling out vital info from images and videos.

- **Pattern recognition**: This is another cool area where AI is making waves. It sifts through massive datasets to spot trends and patterns, helping to pinpoint stuff such as misinformation campaigns or criminal activities way faster and more accurately than a human ever could.

- **Text summarization**: AI can take a ton of text to analyze and keep track of the changing tides of public opinion on various topics.

AI isn't just speeding things up; it's taking data analysis to a whole new level, helping to tackle complex cases and gather information from multiple sources.

Maltego (`https://www.maltego.com`) has come into the spotlight. This tool is a staple in the OSINT utility belt, offering a visual environment that helps in mapping out cyber threats and networks. It's like having a magnifying glass that shows you the details and connects the dots between different pieces of information, giving you a comprehensive view of your investigation landscape.

Whether you're tracking the digital footprint of a person or analyzing cyberattacks, Maltego makes it so stinking easy, offering a range of plugins and transforms that integrate seamlessly with AI functionalities. It's a very useful tool to have in your OSINT toolbox because it enables more in-depth and complex analysis. It gathers various fragments of knowledge and integrates them into one cohesive unit. Its link studies and plain graphs provide a clear image of the relationships between cyber entities, giving the impression that you can practically feel the digital interaction threads spreading out across the canvas. Check out the links and relationships it discovered in the following figure:

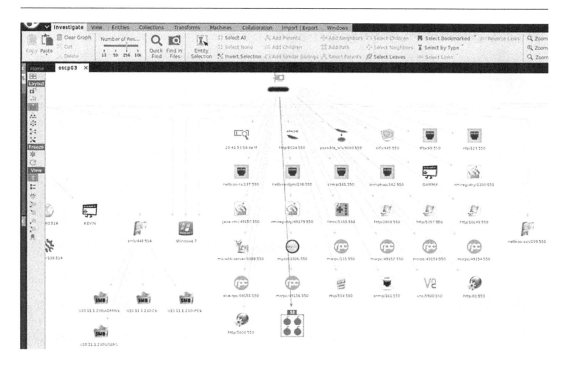

Figure 3.16 – Maltego investigation results

In my personal opinion, AI-powered OSINT isn't just a cool trend; it's going to be a must-have. The old-school ways of gathering intel are just not cutting it anymore, especially with the insane amount of data floating around.

Summary

Now, keep this in mind: the internet is awash with information, but not all of it is golden. It's essential to approach each piece of data like a critical thinker, sifting fact from fiction. Think of it as a form of digital self-defense—before you accept any piece of information as the truth, put it through the wringer of verification. Check it against the trusted sources. This isn't just about being cautious; it's about being smart and not getting tricked. We saw how resources such as images, metadata, and even IoT devices could expose intel about your company or target. Resources that we'd never expect to create exposure. But again, realize that you need to double-check, even triple-check, the intel. So, let's keep our wits about us and remember that in the realm of cyberspace, a little skepticism can go a long way in keeping our information genuine and our conclusions accurate.

In the next chapter, we'll look at various discovery tools and how to find some of those *hidden* gems of data.

Get this book's PDF version and more

Scan the QR code (or go to packtpub.com/unlock). Search for this book by name, confirm the edition, and then follow the steps on the page.

UNLOCK NOW

Note: Keep your invoice handy. Purchases made directly from Packt don't require an invoice.

4

Exploring the Unknown – How Discovery Tools Reveal Hidden Information

This chapter provides an in-depth look at discovery tools and the key utilities that enhance your **Open Source Intelligence (OSINT)** capabilities. These tools are vital for anyone seeking to go beyond basic searches and truly uncover the abundance of information available.

Because discovery tools give you the ability to find data that is either hidden or difficult to locate, they make it possible for you to conduct investigations that are both more comprehensive and perceptive. They are not a luxury but rather a necessity for any OSINT professional. Whether you are looking into potential dangers, investigating the competition in your industry, or just curious about a topic, discovery tools are an absolute must.

In this chapter, we will cover the following:

- Introduction to discovery tools
- Domain and IP address analysis
- Website reconnaissance – Mastering the unseen layers
- Document and metadata analysis
- OSINT data visualization
- Best practices for using discovery tools

By the end of this chapter, you will have a stronger grasp of the role discovery tools play in OSINT. You will know how to utilize them to gather, analyze, and interpret information effectively. You will be well-prepared to take your OSINT skills to the next level.

Let's dive in and explore these essential utilities for elevating your OSINT capabilities.

Introduction to discovery tools

Discovery tools play an invaluable role in OSINT investigations. They allow analysts to uncover hidden information from publicly available data sources that would otherwise remain concealed. OSINT specialists utilize a diverse range of discovery techniques and tools to reveal obscured details, find connections between data, and generate new leads.

There are many types of discovery tools tailored to different investigation needs. Domain and IP address analysis tools peel back the registration details and ownership history of websites and networks. Web scraping and archiving tools extract content, code, and metadata from web pages. Document analysis reveals metadata and other clues hidden within files. Data visualization techniques help illustrate connections within complex OSINT datasets.

Skilled use of discovery tools helps OSINT analysts progress from simple Google searches to excavating profound insights from publicly accessible data. Just as metal detectors can uncover buried treasure, these digital tools surface information that sheds new light on investigations. However, analysts must ensure they are used legally and ethically.

By mastering discovery tools, security professionals can find critical information on people, organizations, locations, and events.

Unlocking network secrets

A digital footprint is a treasure trove of information, a dossier of our digital selves. As the online realm grows, it has become pivotal for individuals and organizations to comprehend the magnitude of the traces they leave behind.

But why does this digital sleuthing matter so much? The answer lies in our interconnected era where data is the new gold. With information comes power—the power to strategize, innovate, and, at times, dominate.

Now that we've seen the big picture of how discovery tools empower OSINT investigations, let's zoom in on one of the most crucial skills in the analyst's toolkit: domain and IP address analysis. It's fascinating how much you can learn about the history and connections of a website just by looking into these details. So, let's get started and take a closer look at how domain and IP address analysis works and why it's such an asset for security professionals

Domain and IP address analysis

Enter **WHOIS**—a mechanism that shines a spotlight on the digital shadows of domain registrations, cutting through the veil of online obscurity. When you navigate a website or send an email, the domain names you encounter are more than mere digital addresses. They are gateways to a repository of details, and WHOIS is the key that unlocks this gateway.

Understanding the DNA of WHOIS – Its definition and purpose

Performing a WHOIS lookup involves sending a query to any of the WHOIS servers responsible for managing the database of the **Top-Level Domain (TLD)**. In response, the WHOIS server looks up the information in its database and then responds with a text record containing the available registration details for that object. This record includes things such as the domain's registrar, registrant contacts, nameservers, registration and expiration dates, and status. Here's exactly what happens:

1. The WHOIS command is invoked. Behind the scenes, your request is routed to a WHOIS server that specializes in the TLD of the domain you're querying. TLDs are `.ccm`, `.org`, and `.net`, or country-specific codes such as `.uk` or `.ca`. Each TLD has its designated WHOIS server.

2. The WHOIS server receives your query and processes it. It then searches its database for information related to the domain name or IP address you provided.

3. If the WHOIS server finds a match, it compiles a response containing various details. This information can include the following:

   - **Registrant information**: The name, address, and contact details of the domain owner.

   - **Registrar information**: The company that registered the domain.

   - **Name servers**: The servers responsible for managing the domain's DNS records.

   - **Creation and expiry dates**: The date the domain was registered and when it expires.

   - **Status**: Whether the domain is active, suspended, or in a different state.

   - **DNSSEC information**: Whether the domain uses DNS Security Extensions for added security. Finally, the data flows back to the terminal, a treasure trove of information laid out for the curious explorer.

4. The WHOIS server formats the information into a structured response and sends it back to your computer. The format can vary depending on the WHOIS server and the TLD but typically resembles plain text.

5. Your computer displays the WHOIS response on your screen. As a cybersecurity professional, you analyze this information to gain insights into the domain's ownership, registration history, and other relevant details.

As I plugged into my terminal, the stark black screen greeted me, waiting for a command. Typing a simple query, I beckoned the beast:

```
whois daledumbsitdown.com
```

The output is shown in the following screenshot:

```
The Registry database contains ONLY .COM, .NET, .EDU domains and
Registrars.
Domain Name: daledumbsitdown.com
Registry Domain ID: 1972026533_DOMAIN_COM-VRSN
Registrar WHOIS Server: whois.registrar.eu
Registrar URL: http://www.registrar.eu
Updated Date: 2023-09-26T19:42:16Z
Creation Date: 2015-10-26T17:41:51Z
Registrar Registration Expiration Date: 2024-10-26T17:41:51Z
Registrar: Hosting Concepts B.V. d/b/a Registrar.eu
Registrar IANA ID: 1647
Registrar Abuse Contact Email: abuse@registrar.eu
Registrar Abuse Contact Phone: +31.104482297
Reseller:
Domain Status: clientTransferProhibited https://icann.org/epp#clientTransferProhibited
Registry Registrant ID: REDACTED FOR PRIVACY
Registrant Name: REDACTED FOR PRIVACY
Registrant Organization: Whois Privacy Protection Foundation
Registrant Street: REDACTED FOR PRIVACY
Registrant City: REDACTED FOR PRIVACY
Registrant State/Province: Zuid-Holland
Registrant Postal Code: REDACTED FOR PRIVACY
```

Figure 4.1 – WHOIS for daledumbsitdown.com

The screen burst into life, revealing lines of data about the domain. It was more than a mere lookup—it was a history, a biography, a fingerprint.

WHOIS isn't just a tool, it serves as the public ledger of the digital estate. At its core, WHOIS provides essential details about a domain or an IP address. Who owns it? When was it registered? When does it expire? It's the pulse of the domain, ticking away in the background, its rhythm often overlooked, but its presence undeniable.

Applicability – Not just domains but IP blocks too

The rabbit hole runs deeper than just domains. Just as every website has its domain, every device on the network has its IP address—a unique set of numbers that distinguishes it from millions of others. Some companies have blocks of IP addresses, which makes things even more interesting as it opens up more information.

When using the WHOIS protocol on IP blocks, you can find out information about their allocation, distribution, and the entities that control them.

Using the IP address of 8.8.8.8, I'm quick to discover the full IP block that belongs to Google.

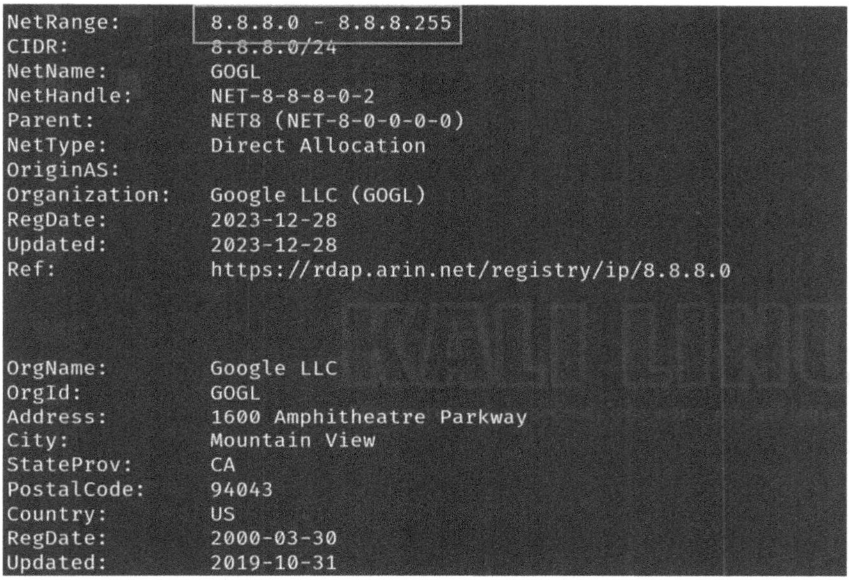

```
NetRange:       8.8.8.0 - 8.8.8.255
CIDR:           8.8.8.0/24
NetName:        GOGL
NetHandle:      NET-8-8-8-0-2
Parent:         NET8 (NET-8-0-0-0-0)
NetType:        Direct Allocation
OriginAS:
Organization:   Google LLC (GOGL)
RegDate:        2023-12-28
Updated:        2023-12-28
Ref:            https://rdap.arin.net/registry/ip/8.8.8.0


OrgName:        Google LLC
OrgId:          GOGL
Address:        1600 Amphitheatre Parkway
City:           Mountain View
StateProv:      CA
PostalCode:     94043
Country:        US
RegDate:        2000-03-30
Updated:        2019-10-31
```

Figure 4.2 – Google's IP block using WHOIS

WHOIS plays a crucial role in mapping the digital landscape. It delineates the borders, records the stories, and guarantees that even though the digital world may seem vast and unpredictable, it never remains uncharted.

The online magnifying glasses – Popular WHOIS lookup platforms

Cyberspace is filled with those who speak the language of WHOIS, but few truly understand its essence. Among the noise, some stand out.

DomainTools

DomainTools (https://www.domaintools.com/) offers a useful WHOIS lookup tool that provides detailed registration information about a domain name. When you enter a domain name into the DomainTools WHOIS search bar, it will display the domain's registration status, registrar info, nameservers, and contact information for the registrant.

Some key info the tool provides includes the following:

- The domain's registration and expiration dates
- The registrar through which the domain is registered
- The registrant's name, phone number, and address
- The administrative and technical contacts for the domain
- The domain's nameservers and DNS information

The DomainTools WHOIS lookup pulls its data from the authoritative WHOIS database for each TLD. It offers a quick and easy way to get a wealth of in-depth data about any domain's ownership and technical details. The tool is useful for domain research, tracking domain registrations, and investigating domains for security purposes.

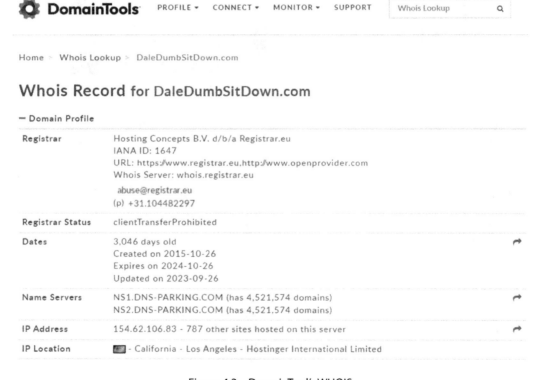

Figure 4.3 – DomainTool's WHOIS

Whois.com

Whois.com is sleek and straightforward. It cuts through the digital fog, laying bare the essence of any domain, without the garnish.

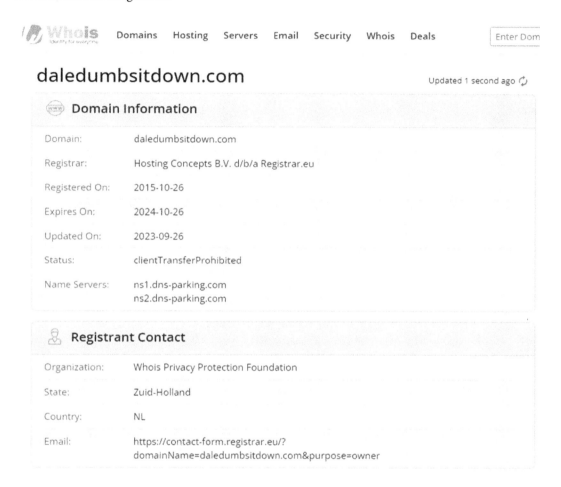

Figure 4.4 – Whois.com's results for daledumbsitdown.com

While WHOIS lookups provide registration details about domain names, many registrants today opt to use privacy or proxy services to hide their personal information from public view. These services replace the registrant's name, address, phone number, and email in the public WHOIS with the contact info of the privacy service instead. This allows domain owners to keep their identities anonymous.

However, it's important to note that their anonymity is not completely guaranteed. Privacy services are legally obligated to disclose the underlying customer data they are protecting if presented with a subpoena or court order. Law enforcement and intellectual property rights holders can petition the courts to override the privacy service and reveal the true domain registrant to identify owners of fraudulent, infringing, or illegal websites through WHOIS data. So, while privacy services offer domain owners more anonymity, their identities can still be uncovered by lawful requests.

If only there was a way to look back in time. You know, maybe back when folks weren't so careful. Oh, wait, there is! The website WHOXY (`https://www.whoxy.com/`) can provide you with a historical listing of a domain. Here's all the juicy stuff on `https://www.daledumbsitdown.com/`:

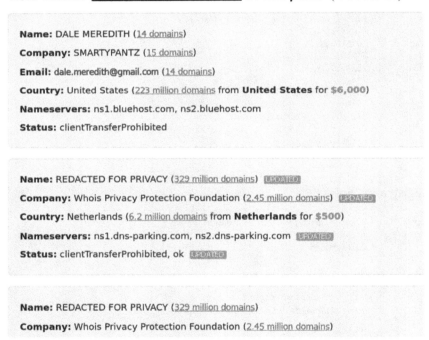

Figure 4.5 – Whoxy.com's results for daledumbsitdown.com

Each tool, with its unique vantage point, allows the intrepid explorer a distinct view into the fabric of the internet. Like different lenses of a microscope, they reveal layers, nuances, and facets otherwise hidden.

Finding the connections

Identifying related domains and ownership connections using WHOIS is a valuable part of cybersecurity investigation, especially when you want to uncover potential links between different online entities. Here's how you can do it:

1. **Start with the primary domain**: Begin by querying the WHOIS database for the primary domain you're interested in. Here is an example:

   ```
   whois daledumbsitdown.com
   ```

   This will provide you with information about the ownership and registration details of the primary domain.

2. **Look for name servers**: In the WHOIS output, look for the domain's name servers. These are the servers responsible for hosting DNS records for the domain. You'll often find entries like the following:

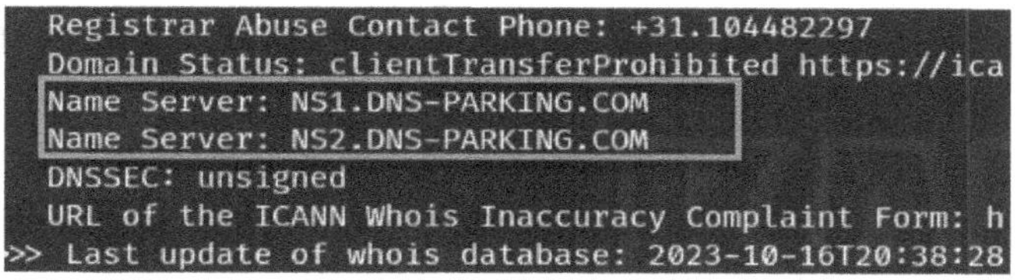

Figure 4.6 – Name servers for daledumbsitdown.com

3. **Investigate name servers**: Now, you'll want to perform WHOIS queries for each of the name servers you've identified. For instance, see the following:

   ```
   whois ns1.dns-parking.com
   whois ns2.dns-parking.com
   ```

> **Note**
>
> These queries will provide information about the name servers themselves and may reveal other domains that use the same name servers. This can be a valuable clue in identifying related domains.

4. **Check for common registrants**: Within the WHOIS results for the name servers, look for common registrants. Registrants are the organizations or individuals who have registered the domains. If you find the same registrant name or contact information across multiple domains, it suggests a potential ownership connection.

5. **Explore subdomains and additional domains**: Beyond name servers, you can also explore subdomains and additional domains associated with the primary domain. Here is an example:

```
whois subdomain.daledumbsitdown.com
whois additional-daledumbsitdown.com
```

The darker side – When attackers use WHOIS

So, picture this: with WHOIS, hackers can go fishing for registration emails and names, which is all part of their grand plan for some targeted phishing shenanigans. I mean, who can resist clicking on an email with a name that seems strangely familiar, right? It's like the perfect bait.

That's not all. These sneaky attackers are also keeping an eagle eye on domains that are about to expire. The moment they see one, they snatch it up faster than you can say "cybersecurity." Why? Well, they might use these hijacked domains to spread malware or redirect innocent web surfers to malicious sites.

But wait, it gets even craftier. By using social engineering tricks, these cyber crooks can actually trick WHOIS contacts into transferring domain ownership. It's like a shady real estate deal in the digital world, letting them hijack websites at will.

Let's not forget about the name servers. WHOIS spills the beans on these critical pieces of the internet's infrastructure, which are just ripe for DDoS attacks or DNS hijacking. With some cleverly forged DNS records, these cyber tricksters can create digital illusions to lead unsuspecting web traffic astray.

To hide their true intentions, attackers often use proxy servers, launching relentless attacks on WHOIS servers to find vulnerabilities and identify their next targets. For them, WHOIS data isn't just a compass; it's a full-blown blueprint for creating chaos.

DNS and IP analysis – Connecting domains to infrastructure

OSINT techniques allow us to leverage DNS and IP data to illuminate hidden connections between domains and infrastructure. For example, a DNS lookup on a domain such as `hackthissite.org` (`dig hackthissite.org`) reveals associated IP addresses:

```
  ┌─(kali⊕kali)-[~]
  └─$ dig hackthissite.org

; <<>> DiG 9.19.17-1-Debian <<>> hackthissite.org
;; global options: +cmd
;; Got answer:
;; ──»HEADER«── opcode: QUERY, status: NOERROR, id: 13300
;; flags: qr rd ra; QUERY: 1, ANSWER: 5, AUTHORITY: 0, ADDITIONAL: 1

;; OPT PSEUDOSECTION:
; EDNS: version: 0, flags:; udp: 512
;; QUESTION SECTION:
;hackthissite.org.              IN      A

;; ANSWER SECTION:
hackthissite.org.       3600    IN      A       137.74.187.102
hackthissite.org.       3600    IN      A       137.74.187.100
hackthissite.org.       3600    IN      A       137.74.187.101
hackthissite.org.       3600    IN      A       137.74.187.104
hackthissite.org.       3600    IN      A       137.74.187.103
```

Figure 4.7 – The output of dig hackthissite.org

We can then perform a reverse DNS lookup on the IP (dig -x 137.74.187.102) to find hostnames associated with that address:

```
  ┌─(kali⊕kali)-[~]
  └─$ dig -x 137.74.187.102

; <<>> DiG 9.19.17-1-Debian <<>> -x 137.74.187.102
;; global options: +cmd
;; Got answer:
;; ──»HEADER«── opcode: QUERY, status: NOERROR, id: 35
;; flags: qr rd ra; QUERY: 1, ANSWER: 1, AUTHORITY: 0, ADDITIONAL: 1

;; OPT PSEUDOSECTION:
; EDNS: version: 0, flags:; udp: 512
;; QUESTION SECTION:
;102.187.74.137.in-addr.arpa.     IN      PTR

;; ANSWER SECTION:
102.187.74.137.in-addr.arpa. 21600 IN   PTR     hackthissite.org.

;; Query time: 220 msec
;; SERVER: 10.10.10.1#53(10.10.10.1) (UDP)
;; WHEN: Mon Oct 16 16:17:15 MDT 2023
;; MSG SIZE  rcvd: 86
```

Figure 4.8 – Dig shows us the PTR for 137.74.187.102

Now, in this case, we don't see any other domains listed because there aren't any others on that host, but in some cases, you might get results like the following:

```
;; ANSWER SECTION:
host1234.examplehosting.com. 3600 IN A 93.184.216.34
site1.com. 3600 IN CNAME host1234.examplehosting.com.
site2.net. 3600 IN CNAME host1234.examplehosting.com.
site3.org. 3600 IN CNAME host1234.examplehosting.com.
```

If you're using a Windows client, your best friend is `nslookup`. Your syntax would be the following:

```
nslookup hackthissite.org
```

The output is as shown in the following screenshot:

Figure 4.9 – nslookup results for hackthissite.org

But wait, there's more!

DNS records provide a wealth of insight for OSINT investigations. By querying various record types, an analyst can illuminate critical details about an organization's internet assets and infrastructure. In this section, we will explore some of the key DNS record types and how to leverage them for useful intelligence.

A and AAAA records

A and **AAAA records** map a domain name to its associated IPv4 and IPv6 addresses respectively. Looking up a domain's A record reveals the IP address hosting the domain, which enables further investigation through reverse DNS lookups and uncovers relationships with other domains hosted on the same IPs.

We can use `nslookup` to query A records:

```
nslookup
> set type=A
> daledumbsitdown.com
```

The output is as shown in the following screenshot:

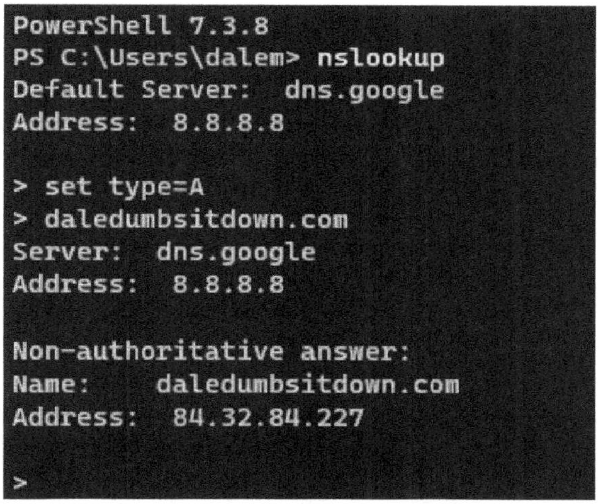

```
PowerShell 7.3.8
PS C:\Users\dalem> nslookup
Default Server:  dns.google
Address:  8.8.8.8

> set type=A
> daledumbsitdown.com
Server:  dns.google
Address:  8.8.8.8

Non-authoritative answer:
Name:     daledumbsitdown.com
Address:  84.32.84.227

>
```

Figure 4.10 – A record lookup for daledumbsitdown.com

MX records

MX or **mail exchange records** specify the designated mail servers for a domain's email delivery. Enumerating a domain's MX records exposes core mail infrastructure that could be targeted in future social engineering or hacking campaigns. We can use a tool such as `nslookup` and have it hyperfocus on specific records. Let's have it find some MX records.

You first type `nslookup` and hit *Enter*:

```
nslookup
> set type=MX
> daledumbsitdown.com
```

The output is as shown in the following screenshot:

```
> set type=mx
> daledumbsitdown.com
Server:  dns.google
Address:  8.8.8.8

Non-authoritative answer:
daledumbsitdown.com        MX preference = 10, mail exchanger = mx2.hostinger.com
daledumbsitdown.com        MX preference = 5, mail exchanger = mx1.hostinger.com
>
```

Figure 4.11 – MX records results using nslookup

This shows two prioritized mail servers for daledumbsitdown.com.

> **Note**
>
> When it comes to priorities, preference = X shows which servers are contacted first. The rule is that the lower the number, the higher the priority, so in this case, the 5 listing (mx1. hostinger.com) is contacted first.

TXT records

TXT records allow freeform text for domain administrators. They are often used to publish configuration data such as SPF records, which identify authorized mail servers for a domain. Gathering SPF data from TXT records reveals approved sending infrastructure for an organization.

```
> set type=txt
> daledumbsitdown.com
Server:  dns.google
Address:  8.8.8.8

Non-authoritative answer:
daledumbsitdown.com        text =

        "google-site-verification=FZnGQZA-xR4TrUjCak_3zyPfhSc8BTM1zVOw2X80LAE"
daledumbsitdown.com        text =

        "v=spf1 include:_spf.mail.hostinger.com ~all"
daledumbsitdown.com        text =

        "pinterest-site-verification=881a39213331c0b4ead786126f31d959"
daledumbsitdown.com        text =

        "google-site-verification=7NNP3Uqgi8cVyDGbcpy8BOGItDFQV1Ug0YFVBsiWlaU"
>
```

Figure 4.12 – TXT record results via nslookup

CNAME records

CNAME or **canonical name records** map an alias domain name to the real domain name. CNAME records can reveal connections between domains and upstream providers.

```
> set type=cname
> hackthissite.org
Server:   dns.google
Address:   8.8.8.8

hackthissite.org
        primary name server = c.ns.buddyns.com
        responsible mail addr = admin.hackthissite.org
        serial  = 2023040305
        refresh = 3600 (1 hour)
        retry   = 900 (15 mins)
        expire  = 604800 (7 days)
        default TTL = 86400 (1 day)
>
```

Figure 4.13 – Shows alias for hackthissite.org.

By leveraging these DNS record types and more, an OSINT investigator can map out the core internet assets and relationships for a target organization or domain. In the next chapter, we will explore additional techniques for gathering infrastructure intelligence.

Mapping the digital footprint – Leveraging DNS and IP analysis

DNS and IP investigation techniques allow us to illuminate an organization's online infrastructure and relationships. Here are some key ways these tools can be applied:

- **Map out a target's infrastructure**: DNS lookups on domains reveal associated IP addresses, name servers, mail servers, and other hosts. Reverse DNS lookups on IPs surface additional connected domains and assets. An analyst can piece these data points together to diagram the target's digital footprint.

- **Identify shared hosting infrastructure**: DNS Lookup often show multiple domains hosted on the same servers or IP space. This can indicate domains owned by the same organization, even if WHOIS details differ.

- **Confirm domain relationships**: DNS analysis validates connections between domains by verifying subnets, name servers, IPs, and other DNS records match. This confirms subsidiary sites, subdomains, affiliate domains, and so on.

- **Spot newly created domains**: Monitoring DNS records over time reveals new domains standing up on existing infrastructure. Useful for tracking new assets.

- **Map infrastructure changes**: Changes in DNS records act as signals for migrations, restructuring, outages, or domain acquisitions.

- **Reveal geographic hosting**: IP geolocation identifies the physical region hosting servers; it provides geographical context.

- **Identify third-party services**: DNS/IP investigation exposes the use of external vendors such as CDNs, DDoS mitigation, and cloud providers based on hostnames.

- **Verify domain legitimacy**: Confirm IP addresses match the real site, not a fake or spoofed domain. This checks validity.

DNS and IP analysis shed light on an organization's online footprint – its infrastructure, relationships, locations, services, and changes. When integrated into the intelligence-gathering process, these techniques can provide invaluable insight into a target's digital presence.

Traceroute and network mapping – Navigating the vast cyber seas

Traversing complex networks can be a daunting task without the right tools. **Traceroute** and **network mapping** are necessary instruments that allow individuals to navigate and understand the intricate pathways of data traffic with precision and clarity. These tools serve as a linchpin, transforming the enigmatic dance of data packets into discernible information.

Traceroute

Traceroute is a network diagnostic tool used to map the path between a source system and a destination system on an IP network. It works by sending UDP or ICMP packets with gradually increasing **Time To Live** (**TTL**) values and recording the source of response packets.

When a traceroute packet is sent, the first hop router decrements the TTL value by 1 and forwards it to the next router. When the TTL value reaches 0, the router that receives 0 as the TTL drops the packet and sends an ICMP time-exceeded message back to the source of the packet.

This allows traceroute to identify each hop along the path by the source IP of the ICMP packet received. It starts with a small TTL, and then increments it to trace each next hop router back to the destination.

For example, a traceroute from Host A to Host B would work like this:

1. Host A sends a UDP packet with a TTL of 1 destined for Host B.
2. The first hop router (R1) receives it, decrements TTL to 0, then drops the packet and sends ICMP back to A. This identifies R1.
3. Host A sends a new packet with a TTL of 2. R1 decrements to 1 and forwards to R2. R2 decrements to 0, drops the packet, and sends ICMP back. This identifies R2.
4. The process continues incrementing the TTL until the destination, Host B, is reached.

Along the way, traceroute (or **tracert** for us Windows folks), records the IP address and latency for each hop. This effectively maps the path and performance between the source and destination on the network. This makes it a powerful troubleshooting and network topology discovery tool.

Traceroute is used from the command line by specifying the destination hostname or IP address. The basic syntax on Linux/Mac is as follows:

```
traceroute destination
```

For example, to trace the route to daledumbsitdown.com, you would input the following:

```
traceroute daledumbsitdown.com
```

This will perform a UDP traceroute and output results like the following:

```
┌──(kali㉿kali)-[~/Desktop]
└─$ traceroute daledumbsitdown.com
traceroute to daledumbsitdown.com (191.96.144.104), 30 hops max,
 1  firewalla.lan (10.10.10.1)  0.365 ms  0.401 ms  0.359 ms
 2  192.168.1.1 (192.168.1.1)  8.908 ms  8.899 ms  8.828 ms
 3  lo0.mar1.slc.xmission.net (166.70.255.53)  11.686 ms  11.642
 4  br2.core.xmission.net (166.70.1.22)  11.490 ms  11.473 ms  1
 5  ae-15.a03.lsanca07.us.bb.gin.ntt.net (129.250.195.105)  45.1
 6  ae-13.r24.lsanca07.us.bb.gin.ntt.net (129.250.3.141)  44.811
 7  ae-3.r22.dllstx14.us.bb.gin.ntt.net (129.250.7.68)  60.907 m
 8  ae-15.r21.dllstx14.us.bb.gin.ntt.net (129.250.2.58)  64.911
 9  ae-4.r25.atlnga05.us.bb.gin.ntt.net (129.250.4.117)  86.958
10  129.250.4.67 (129.250.4.67)  86.739 ms  82.010 ms  81.878 ms
```

Figure 4.14 – Traceroute to daledumbsitdown.com results

Each line lists the hop number, IP address, and latency times. Asterisks indicate no response from that hop.

The asterisks (*) in the traceroute output indicate no response was received from that hop router along the path. There are a few potential reasons for no response:

- **Firewall blocking**: The router may have a firewall that blocks ICMP TTL expired packets or UDP/TCP traceroute packets. This prevents it from returning a response.

- **Rate limiting**: To prevent overload, some routers rate limit how many traceroute packets they will respond to. If the limit is reached, it will stop responding.

- **Packet loss**: Network congestion or packet drops along the path can result in the traceroute packet being lost before reaching that hop. Thus, no reply is generated.

- **Invalid address**: The router IP may be misconfigured or unreachable, so the traceroute packet never arrives to generate a response.

- **Router outage**: The router could be down, offline, or otherwise unavailable to handle the traceroute packet and return a reply.

We can also specify TCP traceroute using -T, the number of hops with -m, and perform a reverse path trace with -r flags:

```
traceroute -T -m 50 -r daledumbsitdown.com
```

This executes a TCP traceroute limiting the output to 50 max hops and tracing the path in reverse from destination to source.

Network mapping

Network mapping is a vital technique in the OSINT toolkit for unraveling the digital footprint of a target organization. OSINT analysts leverage various tools to visually map network paths, identify critical infrastructure, and detect relationships between internet-connected assets.

Nmap

Nmap allows active probing of live hosts to enumerate services and operating systems. Here is an example:

```
nmap 192.168.1.1
```

Performs a basic SYN scan on the host to find open TCP ports:

```
nmap -sU -p 123,161 10.0.0.0/24
```

UDP scan targeting SNMP on a subnet.

Looking to figure out which OS is running on a target? See the following:

```
nmap -O hackthissite.org
```

Or, if you want to dig deeper and a little sneakier, you can use "stealth" mode:

```
nmap -sS hackthissite.org
```

When it comes to using Nmap, you could write whole books about this awesome tool. In fact, there are several titles of Nmap here at Packt Publishing.

Wireshark

Wireshark is an open source packet analyzer that enables deep inspection of network traffic, communications, and protocols. Acting as a multipurpose network microscope, the tool allows users to capture packets flowing through wired, wireless, and virtual interfaces. This is another tool that has its own book written about it! Let's start by following these steps:

1. Start Wireshark and begin capturing packets on the desired interface. Apply a display filter such as ip.addr==154.41.250.193 to isolate traffic to/from the target IP.

2. Inspect the captured packets and take note of any other IP addresses communicating with the target. These may be servers, clients, or adjacent routers.

3. Apply additional filters to isolate traffic from the discovered IPs. For example, apply `ip.src==192.168.1.105` to view all traffic from a newly found IP.

4. Analyze the traffic and determine hostnames via DNS requests/responses. Identify open ports based on destination ports, and determine services via protocol analysis.

5. Right-click on communications streams and select **Follow TCP Stream** to reconstruct flows and uncover any readable packet data that may provide clues about function and purpose.

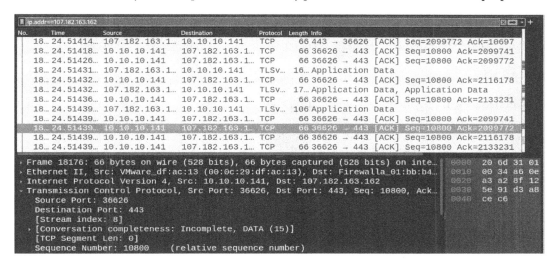

Figure 4.15 – Looking at the connections to daledumbsitdown.com via Wireshark

Leverage Wireshark's filtering, TCP analysis, and decoding capabilities to expand the network map starting from `154.41.250.193`. Discover new IPs, hostnames, relationships, and role details for adjacent hosts.

Supplement Wireshark analysis with external lookups such as reverse DNS, WHOIS, and Nmap scans to enrich the discovered IP and hostname data.

We've just seen how Wireshark can be a powerful ally in uncovering the layers of network communication and the secrets they hold. But our exploration doesn't stop there. With the network landscape mapped out, it's time to shift our focus to website reconnaissance.

Website reconnaissance – Mastering the unseen layers

Website reconnaissance with Kali Linux provides users with an extensive array of tools designed for detailed analysis and information gathering.

In the following section, we'll delve into the toolkit offered by Kali Linux for website reconnaissance. You'll learn how to scrape websites for data, analyze metadata with **Metagoofil**, revisit site history with the **Wayback Machine**, and probe for hidden directories and files. These techniques form the core of our web analysis, providing a well-rounded approach to uncovering online insights

Web page scraping and analysis

Web page scraping refers to the automated extraction and harvesting of data from websites. It involves using tools and scripts to systematically retrieve and process content, metadata, and other information from web pages.

Web scraping enables the large-scale gathering of textual content, images, documents, and structured data from across the internet. This raw data can then be analyzed to uncover hidden insights, monitor changes over time, feed datasets, and various other applications.

Now that we've seen how web scraping helps us collect a wide array of information, let's look at Metagoofil.

Metagoofil

While metadata can provide useful information about a document, its presence can also pose a significant security risk. When documents containing metadata are published online or shared broadly, that sensitive information becomes exposed. Savvy attackers can harvest this metadata through OSINT techniques, using it for nefarious purposes.

This is where a tool like Metagoofil comes in handy. Metagoofil allows you to harvest metadata from documents published on websites, providing insight into an organization's users, software, and more. The harvested metadata can then be used for various security research and testing purposes, like the following:

- Designing more effective social engineering attacks
- Discovering software versions to search for potential exploits
- Identifying specific employee names and email addresses

While Metagoofil used to be included in Kali Linux by default, at some point it might get removed from the standard build (it happens, folks). However, the good news is that you can always easily download and install it using the `apt-get` command.

Open a terminal and run the following:

```
sudo apt-get install metagoofil
```

Now that we have Metagoofil installed, let's put it to use harvesting some metadata. For this example, we'll gather metadata from SANS.org, a popular cybersecurity education site.

Here's the command we'll run:

```
metagoofil -d packtpub.com -t doc,pdf -l 20 -n 10 -o packt -f html
```

Let's break this down:

- `-d packtpub.com` specifies the target domain
- `-t doc,pdf` defines the file types to search for
- `-l 20` limits the search to 20 results
- `-n 10` limits the file downloads to 10
- `-o scans` sets the output directory as `packt`
- `-f html` formats the output as HTML

After a minute or two, Metagoofil will start printing results to the terminal.

```
┌──(kali㉿kali)-[~]
└─$ metagoofil -d packtpub.com -t doc,pdf -l 20 -n 10 -o packt -f hmtl
[*] Searching for 20 .doc files and waiting 30.0 seconds between searches
[*] Results: 0 .doc files found
[*] Searching for 20 .pdf files and waiting 30.0 seconds between searches
[*] Results: 20 .pdf files found
https://www.packtpub.com/sites/default/files/downloads/65720T_ColoredImages.pdf
https://www.packtpub.com/sites/default/files/downloads/Reinforcement_Learning.pdf
https://www.packtpub.com/sites/default/files/downloads/84200T_Bonus_Chapter.pdf
https://www.packtpub.com/sites/default/files/downloads/29010S_ColoredImages.pdf
```

Figure 4.16 – Using Metagoofil to scrap .doc and .pdf from packtpub.com

To view the results in a more organized way, we can open the HTML output in `/root/packt/index.html`. This gives us a cleanly formatted table with the metadata extracted from the documents. In some cases, Metagoofil might find software or even emails. It's kind of cool.

Now, I know what you're thinking; we've all been there – happily scraping along until Google suddenly starts throwing HTTP 429 errors, blocking your IP for making too many requests. Annoying! But with the right tools, you can dance around these blocks and keep scraping. The key is proxies.

First, grab proxychains to manage routing through multiple proxies. Just install it on your Linux system with the following code:

```
sudo apt install proxychains4 -y
```

Next, set up the proxychains configuration file at `/etc/proxychains4.conf`. Enable the `round_robin` mode to cycle through different proxies randomly:

```
vim /etc/proxychains4.conf
round_robin
chain_len = 1
proxy_dns
remote_dns_subnet 224
tcp_read_time_out 15000
tcp_connect_time_out 8000
[ProxyList]
socks4 [list the ip of your proxy and port]
socks4 [list the ip of your proxy and port]
```

> **Note**
>
> The format here is something like this: `socks4 192.168.0.1 8000`. Again, the more proxies, the better.

Metagoofil will smoothly rotate through the proxies, allowing you to scrape for longer without being shut down. You may even be able to decrease the scrape delay since you'll have many IPs in rotation. Just respect site terms, data limits, and `robots.txt`, and scrape ethically across the web. With proxychains, you can avoid blocks and extract data uninterrupted.

Analysis and insight

With the data procured, the next step hinges on analysis. Tools such as **grep** can be employed to sift through the content, searching for specific patterns, keywords, or data of interest. The capability to filter and pinpoint information elevates the process from mere data collection to insightful analysis:

```
grep -ri "pattern" /path/to/downloaded/website/data
```

I know that's a lot, so let's break this command down a bit:

- `grep`: This is a command-line utility used for searching text patterns within files. It stands for **global regular expression print**.
- `-ri`: These are options provided to grep:
  - `-r` (or `--recursive`): This option tells grep to search for the pattern not only in the specified directory but also in all its subdirectories.
  - `-i` (or `--ignore-case`): This option makes the search case-insensitive, so it will match "Pattern," "pattern," "pAtTeRn," and so on.

- `"pattern"`: This is the text pattern you want to search for within the files. You would replace `"pattern"` with the actual text you're looking for.

- `/path/to/downloaded/website/data`: This is the directory where you want to start the search. The `-r` option ensures that grep searches this directory and all its subdirectories.

So, when you run this command, it will search for the specified `pattern` within all the text files in the `/path/to/downloaded/website/data` directory and its subdirectories, and it will print any matching lines it finds.

Wayback Machine and web archives

The Wayback Machine allows you to explore how websites looked in the past. It stores periodic snapshots of sites over time, providing access to old versions of pages and content that may no longer exist on the live web.

This archive can be incredibly useful for web scraping and OSINT purposes:

- **Access deleted or changed web content**: The Wayback Machine has versions of pages that are no longer available. You can scrape content that has been removed from sites.

- **Analyze website changes**: Compare different versions of a site's code and structure over time to identify changes.

- **Research domains**: View historic ownership records, sites associated with emails or names, and predecessor domains.

- **Discover hidden or forgotten sites**: The archive contains sites long gone from the live web. You can uncover hidden gems.

- **Build datasets**: Extract data from current and historical sources in bulk.

Unearthing hidden insights

Each URL archived is a piece of the intricate puzzle, offering insights into a website's security posture, content evolution, and structural changes. By analyzing this data, one can identify patterns, uncover vulnerabilities, and gain insights that are often concealed in the real-time version of the website.

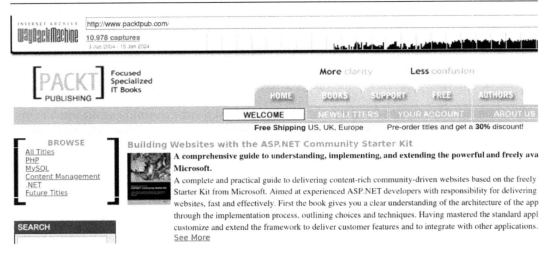

Figure 4.17 – Packt's first webpage from 2004

The retrospective analysis facilitated by the Wayback Machine is integral in assessing the security landscape of a website. It enables professionals to understand historical vulnerabilities, track fixes, and anticipate potential future threats. Each archive, each URL is an asset, contributing to the comprehensive analysis that shapes informed, strategic cybersecurity decisions.

Directory and file enumeration

Websites contain all kinds of unpublished directories and files with useful info – their hidden gems. Security researchers have a sweet tool called **DirBuster** (`https://gitlab.com/kalilinux/packages/dirbuster`) to uncover these hidden goods. DirBuster works by forcing requests across a site using smart wordlists to dig up stuff website owners don't want to be found. It tries tons of file paths and directory names from its wordlists, looking for any that return real results instead of errors.

When DirBuster scores a hit, it logs these secret paths for you to check out later. These discoveries often lead to private assets the site owners buried far down in the structure, thinking no one would ever look there.

To really dig deep into a site, you need persistence and solid wordlists tailored to that site. DirBuster will methodically poke, prod, and excavate the site's innards to expose these concealed digital assets. It's like an archaeological dig, revealing all the website's unpublished treasures.

Launching and utilizing DirBuster is a straightforward process. Its intuitive GUI aids users in setting parameters effectively, ensuring a comprehensive search that is as exhaustive as it is precise.

Start DirBuster from the terminal by typing the following:

```
dirbuster
```

And boom, the GUI will appear:

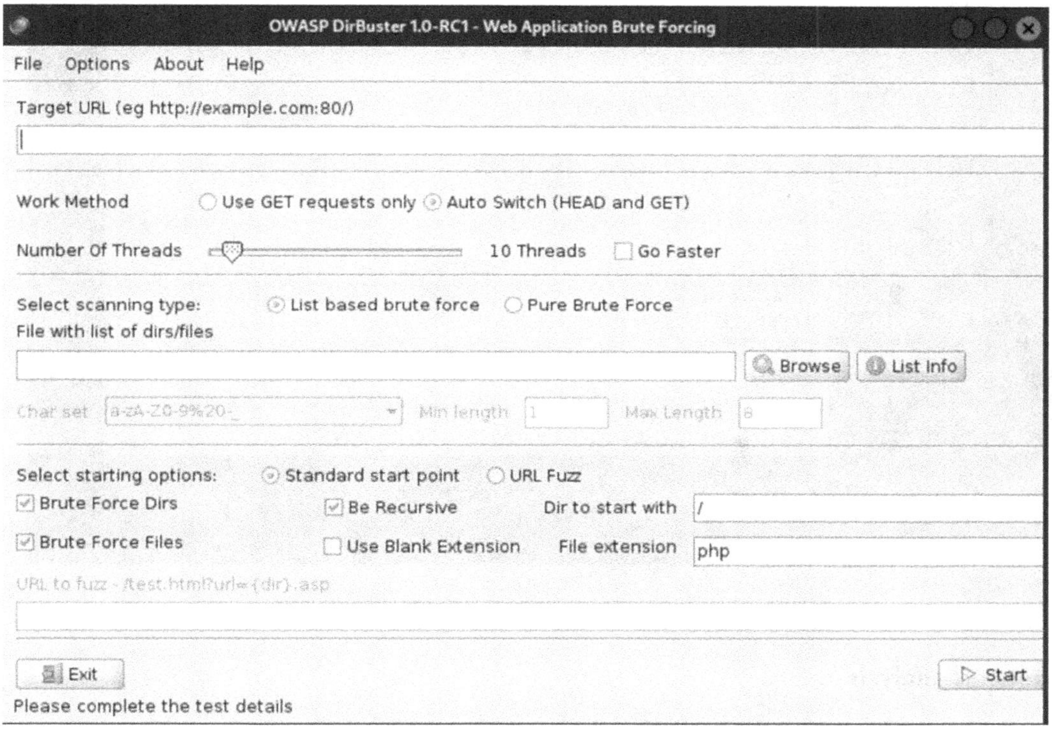

Figure 4.18 – The DirBuster interface in Kali

Configuring DirBuster involves setting the target URL and selecting an appropriate wordlist, like the one located at `/usr/share/wordlists/dirbuster/directory-list-lowercase-2.3-medium.txt`. The selected wordlist and the defined file extensions steer the search, transforming DirBuster into a silent seeker of hidden digital alleys and vaults.

Hit the **Start** button and just like you see in the following figure, DirBuster starts doing its thing:

Figure 4.19 – DirBuster scanning daledumbsitdown.com

robots.txt analysis

Complementing DirBuster, the analysis of the `robots.txt` file serves as a preliminary step to understand the sections of a website that are intentionally kept away from search engine indexing. The `robots.txt` file is a standard used by websites to communicate instructions to web robots and crawlers about which pages/files the site owner wants to be blocked from indexing or accessing. Here are some key points about `robots.txt`:

- It is a text file that must be written exactly as `robots.txt` and placed in the root directory of a website

- It contains a set of rules indicating which user agents (bots/crawlers) are allowed or disallowed from accessing pages on the site

- The rules use the robots exclusion standard format

To take a look at a given `robots.txt` file, try this out:

```
curl -s https://www.apple.com/robots.txt | less
```

You should see a similar result in the following screenshot as a result, which shows some directory structures that search engines shouldn't crawl.

Figure 4.20 – Output showing directory structures not crawled by search engines

This returns the contents of the `robots.txt` file in a more readable format, which unlocks the secrets of the website's hidden corners. The paths and directories listed here can be further explored to glean insights into potentially sensitive or confidential sections of the website.

Harmonizing DirBuster and robots.txt

By integrating the precise, brute-force capability of DirBuster with the initial insights gleaned from `robots.txt` analysis, investigators ensure a two-pronged approach to unearthing hidden data. Where `robots.txt` provides the initial map, DirBuster is the explorer, trekking the uncharted paths to unveil what lies beyond the visible – unveiling data, assets, and configurations often integral to comprehensive website analysis and security assessment.

The confluence of DirBuster's rigorous search and the foundational insights from `robots.txt` crafts a comprehensive pathway into the concealed layers of a website, each tool contributing to painting a holistic picture of the website's architecture and content distribution.

> **Note**
> Remember the superhero pledge: *"With great power, comes great responsibility."* And my phrase: *"Just because you can, doesn't mean you should."*

So, we've had a good time with directory and file enumeration, finding what's tucked away on a website. Next up, we're going to switch gears a bit and dive into the world of documents and metadata analysis. It's like taking a closer look at the details behind the details, and it can tell us a whole lot more about the information we've found.

Document and metadata analysis

Documents and their associated metadata often resemble hidden gems, each encapsulating a wealth of information frequently overlooked. Files such as PDFs, Word documents, and spreadsheets not only carry explicit content but are also imbued with metadata that reveals details such as authorship, creation and modification dates, and sometimes, sensitive information unintended for public view.

Identifying hidden information in documents and files

The revelation of concealed information within documents and digital files is akin to unearthing hidden treasures. These concealed pieces of data, intentionally or unintentionally embedded, can offer profound insights into the realms of cybersecurity, forensic investigation, and beyond. Kali Linux, adorned with a rich suite of tools, stands as an indispensable ally for professionals in this endeavor.

Strategic metadata extraction

Each file format carries its unique set of metadata, and understanding how to extract this data efficiently is key. Investigators need to be adept at using the right tool for the right file format, ensuring that the extracted metadata is comprehensive and accurate.

With this refined skillset, professionals are not just uncovering data; they are weaving through the intricate threads of digital files and documents, each piece of metadata a clue, leading to profound insights, revelations, and discoveries that define the pinnacle of OSINT investigations.

FOCA

I've got an awesome tool for you – check out **FOCA**, which is short for **Fingerprinting Organizations with Collected Archives** (`https://github.com/ElevenPaths/FOCA`), and is for grabbing documents from websites and analyzing the metadata inside them. Metadata is like the hidden data about a file – it can contain juicy details such as the usernames of people who edited the doc, software versions used to make it, file paths showing where it's stored, and more neat insider info!

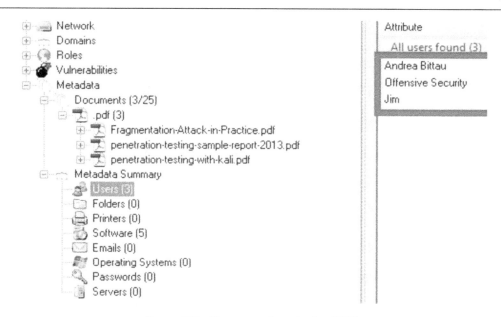

Figure 4.21 – Usernames found using FOCA

While there are probably some more advanced tools out there, FOCA is free and super easy to use on Windows systems. It works by quietly searching through Google, Bing, and DuckDuckGo for various document types such as Word docs, PDFs, Excel spreadsheets, PowerPoint presentations – anything it can find from your target domain. And the best part is it does this passively in the background without making a lot of noise to alert the site you're poking around.

All the metadata that FOCA extracts can provide valuable clues and pivot points for further investigation, which is where the real fun begins! For instance, you can take the usernames it finds and search for them on other platforms to see if they're associated with that person elsewhere online. Or, you can look up the software versions in the metadata and check if they have any known vulnerabilities that could be leveraged by someone with less-than-stellar intentions. The possibilities to explore are nearly endless!

Analyzing document contents for valuable clues

Key points and facts buried in files such as PDFs, Office documents, text files, and more may provide critical clues about an organization or individual's activities, plans, partners, and more. Techniques such as text extraction, metadata analysis, and passage flagging can systematically surface key names, dates, locations, incidents, and other details that may have been overlooked when initially reviewing a document. Furthermore, documents often contain hidden metadata such as geolocation, authorship information, and edits that can provide context around its creation and distribution. Thoroughly mining the textual content and metadata within documents collected during OSINT operations enables analysts to uncover subtle clues and assemble a more complete intelligence picture.

So, we've collected some interesting details from our document sleuthing—names, dates, places, you name it. Now, it's time to take all those pieces we've gathered and see the bigger picture. That's where OSINT data visualization steps in. By turning our findings into visuals, we're not just making sense of the data; we're setting the stage to uncover the "*aha!*" moments with ease and insight.

OSINT data visualization

OSINT data visualization is the process of transforming raw, complex data into interactive and understandable visual formats. It involves using various tools and techniques to create graphs, heatmaps, network diagrams, and other visual representations that make patterns, trends, and insights easily identifiable. In the world of OSINT, data visualization is crucial to interpreting large volumes of data and extracting meaningful intelligence. Through this practice, analysts can quickly discern connections, anomalies, and valuable information that would be challenging to understand in raw, text-based formats.

But why is visualization so pivotal, so quintessential to OSINT?

- **Clarity and comprehension**: Visualization brings clarity. It turns abstract, complex data into tangible, interpretable visuals where patterns emerge, trends unveil, and insights stand naked, bared for the observer to see, to understand.

- **Efficiency and speed**: Time visualization is a mechanism that allows me, the observer, the analyst, to sift through mountains of data with efficiency, to discern patterns with speed, and to arrive at insights with a swiftness that raw data analysis could never afford.

- **Decision-making and action**: Decisions are as pivotal as the data that informs them. Visualization connects data to decisions and insights to actions. Each visual is a lens, magnifying the intricate, often obscured details, offering a clarity that becomes the foundation upon which decisions, actions, and reactions are anchored.

Here I am at my computer, surrounded by piles of OSINT scraps I've collected. As I stare at this heap of social profiles, public records, and website code, I'm getting that feeling in my gut that data visualization is about to turn these random bits into epic discoveries!

The real power of data visualization lies in its capacity to surface hidden insights and crystallize significance from subtle whispers in the noise. As abstract data points transform into rich relationship webs, activity timelines, geographic maps, and statistical charts, their meaning is synthesized into revelation.

Tools and techniques for visualizing OSINT data

Navigating OSINT requires tools and techniques to uncover hidden insights. Here are some of my favorite tools, some of which we'll look at in more detail in the next chapter:

- **Maltego**: Maltego (`https://www.maltego.com/`) creates a graph model of how various entities such as people, websites, domains, IP addresses, organizations, and more are connected together.

Figure 4.22 – Maltego showing links to email and name for LinkedIn.com

Linkages are discovered through transforms that automate searching, filtering, and correlating data from both open and proprietary sources. This one is my personal favorite.

- **Gephi**: Gephi is an open source graph and network analysis toolkit written in Java. It is commonly used for analyzing and visualizing connections within networks such as social networks, infrastructure maps, relationship graphs, and more. Gephi is available for free download at `https://gephi.org` and runs on Windows, Mac, and Linux systems.

- **CaseFile**: What is Maltego CaseFile? Let me tell you a story. Imagine you're a cyber investigator rummaging through mounds of offline data collected across various cases – spreadsheets of financial transactions, phone records, suspicious emails, you name it. How do you make sense of all this intel? That's where CaseFile comes in. CaseFile lets you take piles of offline data and whip up visual relationship maps faster than you can drink your morning cup of joe.

CaseFile opens a world where offline data comes alive, connecting dots and unveiling patterns without internet connectivity.

These OSINT tools, each utilizing unique techniques, transform obscure codes and ambiguous data into a symphony of illuminating visualizations.

Best practices for using discovery tools

Data is alive, not just in existence, but in a constant state of evolution and because of that, the tools of yesterday can quickly become the relics of tomorrow. Every day, as I plunge into the depths of OSINT, I am reminded that vigilance is not just desirable; it's indispensable. I've formed a habit or ritual for myself. There is always a search for the newest, best, and most advanced tools and methods for discovery. For me, RSS feeds, forums, and community boards are more than just platforms; they're the lifelines and silent guardians that keep me up to date on how OSINT tools are changing.

I usually tell folks to start by using multiple tools rather than relying on just one. Each tool has unique strengths in searching different sources, whether social media, public records, or technical databases. So, I leverage different tools accordingly to get a more comprehensive picture.

It's also important to vary up your search keywords using synonyms, related terms, misspellings – anything to uncover as many angles as possible. Also take advantage of built-in filters to narrow down results by date, location, and source type – that's crucial for pinpointing the most relevant data.

Once you start getting results, it's critical to evaluate the credibility and potential bias of each source. Consider things such as the authority, reputation, and corroborating evidence available. Also, be thoughtful about organizing your findings using mind maps, link charts, and timelines to spotlight connections.

Oh, and don't forget to cover your tracks – use proxies, VPNs, and anonymous accounts so targets can't detect your activity. You obviously need to respect platforms' terms of service and local privacy laws, too. Ethics are a huge part of OSINT in my book.

There's a ton more we could get into, such as monitoring changes to your targets, securing your own activities, and continuously expanding your skills. However, following best practices such as vetting sources, varying keywords, organizing data, and digging ethically will put you on the right path to OSINT success.

Summary

By now, you should be packed and primed with new OSINT discovery superpowers! We went on a hands-on tour of how to dig hidden gems out of domains, IP records, websites, documents – you name it. With your new toolbelt of detection techniques, you can transform scattered dots into vivid narratives. So, get out there and sleuth away.

Up next, we'll get into more tools that help to automate some of our OSINT data gathering as well as a look at a cool operating system designed around OSINT engagements.

5

From Recon-ng to Trace Labs – A Tour of the Best Open Source Intelligence Tools

This chapter is designed to be your companion in navigating the rich ecosystem of some additional **Open Source Intelligence** (**OSINT**) tools that can unlock vast troves of data hidden in plain sight on the internet. From cybersecurity professionals to investigative journalists, understanding and utilizing these tools is crucial for sifting through the digital expanse to collect relevant information.

In this chapter, we'll discuss the following:

- Recon-ng – A powerful OSINT framework
- Maltego – Visualizing OSINT data and connections
- Shodan – The search engine for the **Internet of Things** (**IoT**)
- Trace Labs – A powerful OS designed just for OSINT
- Overview of the Aircrack-ng suite
- Additional open source OSINT tools
- Keeping up with the open source OSINT landscape

By the end of this chapter, you'll be familiar with even more OSINT tools that can enhance your research capabilities. You'll also gain a little hands-on experience with these popular tools.

Recon-ng – A powerful OSINT framework

Recon-ng is a slick web reconnaissance framework that has some seriously useful features to improve your intel game. It's built using a modular architecture, so you can easily expand its capabilities by installing new modules from the built-in marketplace. The community keeps developing fresh modules to keep Recon-ng on the cutting edge.

It also uses an interactive command-line interface that makes the tool a breeze to use, even for newbies. But don't let the easy interface fool you – Recon-ng has some powerful data management abilities, automatically storing scraped information in a structured database for easy retrieval and exporting.

The bottom line is that Recon-ng combines a flexible modular architecture, community-driven marketplace, intuitive interface, robust data management, and API expandability to make it a seriously powerful framework for open source web reconnaissance.

Here's how to install and set up Recon-ng on Kali Linux:

1. Open your Terminal.
2. Clone the Recon-ng repository with the following command:

    ```
    git clone https://github.com/lanmaster53/recon-ng.git
    ```

3. Navigate to the cloned directory:

    ```
    cd recon-ng
    ```

4. Install the required dependencies:

    ```
    pip3 install -r REQUIREMENTS
    ```

5. Launch Recon-ng:

    ```
    ./recon-ng
    ```

If you want to install it on Windows, well, that's easy too:

1. First, you need Python in your arsenal. Recon-ng is developed in Python, and it's best compatible with Python 2.7.x. You can download it from the official Python website. During installation, check the **Add Python to PATH** option, which is like setting up a map for your system to locate Python easily.

2. Once installed, open your Command Prompt (you can search for cmd in the Start menu) and type python --version. This step is like checking your gear before a mission. You should see the Python version displayed, confirming that Python is ready for action.

3. With Python set up, it's time to install Recon-ng. In the same Command Prompt window, enter the following command:

    ```
    pip install recon-ng
    ```

4. This is akin to loading your digital toolbox with a specialized tool. Python's package manager, `pip`, will handle the installation, fetching all necessary components like a skilled quartermaster.

Now, you're ready to launch:

```
recon-ng
```

Now, I didn't forget the macOS folks. Installing Recon-ng on macOS involves a slightly different set of steps compared to Windows. It's akin to preparing for a different kind of cybersecurity expedition, where the terrain (operating system) requires a unique set of tools and preparations.

Here's how to install Recon-ng on macOS:

1. First, you'll need Homebrew, the package manager for macOS. It's like a Swiss Army knife for software installation on a Mac. Open the Terminal (you can find it in **Applications | Utilities**) and run the following command:

```
/bin/bash -c "$(curl -fsSL https://raw.githubusercontent.com/
Homebrew/install/HEAD/install.sh)"
```

This command downloads and runs the Homebrew installation script, setting up Homebrew on your system.

2. macOS usually comes with Python pre-installed; it's usually an older version. You'll need Python 2.7 for Recon-ng. Install it using Homebrew by typing the following command:

```
brew install python@2
```

3. To ensure Python is installed correctly, type `python2 --version` in the Terminal. This should display the Python version, confirming that the right tool is in place.

4. Now, with Python ready, install Recon-ng using `pip`, Python's package manager. In the Terminal, enter the following command:

```
pip2 install recon-ng
```

This command tells `pip` to fetch Recon-ng and install it, much like how you'd download the latest security patches for your systems.

After the installation, it's time to launch Recon-ng. Simply type `recon-ng` in your Terminal. This is akin to booting up a sophisticated security program, ready to delve into the depths of cyber reconnaissance.

After the installation is complete, you're almost ready to dive into the digital reconnaissance field.

Running modules and gathering information with Recon-ng

The framework combines a plethora of tools and techniques, streamlining them into an organized system of modules. Each module, ranging from domain profiling to social media scraping, is crafted to provide specific information about a target.

After installing Recon-ng, we want to make sure you understand the workspaces; these are essential.

To create a new workspace, use the following command:

```
workspaces create [workspace_name]
```

The output is as follows:

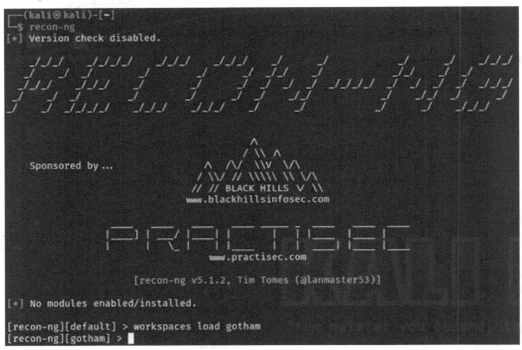

Figure 5.1 – Loading a workspace called gotham

Utilizing a workspace in Recon-ng is akin to setting up a dedicated project folder on your computer. Recon-ng's workspace functionality allows users to separate the data and configurations of different projects. This compartmentalization is crucial for several reasons:

- **Isolation of projects**: Each workspace in Recon-ng acts as an isolated container for a project's data. This means that when you're working on multiple investigations or tasks, each one can have its own workspace with its respective data, modules, and configurations. There's no risk of cross-contamination between projects, which is a cardinal rule for any good investigation.

- **Maintaining focus**: By segmenting data into workspaces, you can maintain a clear focus on the task at hand without distraction from unrelated data. This is especially important when working with large amounts of information, as it helps avoid confusion and ensures that you're only seeing what's relevant to your current inquiry.

- **Data integrity and non-interference**: Using separate workspaces helps preserve the integrity of your data. For example, if you need to revisit a previous project for additional analysis or to verify findings, you can be confident that the data has remained untouched by other activities.

- **Efficient reporting**: When it's time to compile findings into a report, having all relevant data within a single workspace streamlines the process. There's no need to sift through unrelated information, and you can export or reference the findings from that workspace directly.

- **Collaborative flexibility**: If you work in a team, workspaces can be shared among team members, allowing for collaboration without risking the alteration of personal or other project data. Each member can switch between workspaces as needed, working in parallel on different aspects of the same project or on entirely separate projects.

Then, we have modules. The built-in marketplace has tons of modules available covering a wide range of reconnaissance tactics. Finding what you need is a cinch with the search feature, and installing new modules is as simple as typing `marketplace install [module]`.

> **Note**
> Adding API keys is a snap too. Just use the `keys add [name] [value]` command to start leveraging services such as Shodan. Powerful!

Understanding and effectively using module commands is like knowing how to navigate through a complex security system, each command serving a specific purpose in your cybersecurity toolkit. Let's take a closer look at this:

- **Searching for modules**:

  To search the marketplace for a module, you can type the following:

  ```
  marketplace search
  ```

- **Viewing available modules**:

  The following command will display categories and modules. You'll see domain-based, location-based, and several other modules, each serving a unique purpose:

  ```
  show modules
  ```

- **Choosing and using a module**:

  To download and install a module from the marketplace, type the following:

  ```
  marketplace install [name of the module]
  ```

Then, to load the `modules load hackertarget` module type (or whatever the module name is you installed):

```
[recon-ng][gotham] > marketplace install hackertarget
[*] Module installed: recon/domains-hosts/hackertarget
[*] Reloading modules ...
[recon-ng][gotham] > modules load hackertarget
[recon-ng][gotham][hackertarget] > 
```

Figure 5.2 – Commands that install and load a module from the marketplace

- **Setting the necessary options for the module**:

   First, to see what options are available, you can type the following:

   ```
   options lists
   ```

   Each module has specific options you'll need to configure. Commonly, this will involve setting a target such as a domain name or IP address. So, I'm going to type the following:

   ```
   options set SOURCE example.com
   ```

- **Running the module**:

   With options set, you're ready to execute, so type the following command. The module will then do its magic, pulling the information it was designed to retrieve:

   ```
   run
   ```

   Once the module completes its operation, you can view the stored results with this command:

   ```
   show [table_name]
   ```

   For example, to view hosts you've discovered, type the following:

   ```
   show hosts
   ```

   The output would be something like this:

```
[recon-ng][gotham][hackertarget] > show hosts

+------+--------------------------------+------------------+
| rowid |            host                |    ip_address    |
+------+--------------------------------+------------------+
|  1   | data.packtpub.com              | 52.215.120.22    |
|  2   | salesdb.packtpub.com           | 83.166.169.242   |
|  3   | hub.packtpub.com               | 172.67.31.83     |
|  4   | datahub.packtpub.com           | 172.67.31.83     |
|  5   | epic.packtpub.com              | 52.19.26.156     |
|  6   | staging-epic.packtpub.com      | 52.48.37.122     |
|  7   | dev-epic.packtpub.com          | 52.18.34.177     |
|  8   | subscription-rc.packtpub.com   | 172.67.31.83     |
|  9   | dtc.packtpub.com               | 192.168.0.110    |
```

Figure 5.3 – Output of Recon-ng against packtpub.com

The beauty of Recon-ng lies in this iterative approach, where each cycle of reconnaissance potentially unveils more details about your target. Recon-ng's vast module library is its core asset. While the preceding steps provide a generic overview, each module may have its unique nuances. Regularly explore the available modules and stay updated with the Recon-ng marketplace for new additions.

Maltego – Visualizing OSINT data and connections

Maltego is a tool used in cybersecurity to visualize and link data, helping experts uncover and understand online relationships and networks. It's handy for tracking digital activities and analyzing cyber threats.

What sets Maltego apart is its ability to aggregate multiple reconnaissance tasks into a cohesive interface. Moreover, Kali Linux users have the added advantage of accessing a community edition, which offers an array of scans without any initial cost.

With Maltego, users can extract a wide range of information: personal details such as names, emails, and aliases; organizational data, including companies and websites; internet infrastructure details such as domains, IP addresses, and associated networks; documentation and files.

Major government agencies, including the United States **National Security Agency** (**NSA**), also employ tools such as Maltego to map out connections and monitor potential threats effectively.

Getting started with Maltego for OSINT investigations

Maltego is a pivotal tool in the OSINT sphere, designed primarily for data visualization. By presenting complex data in a more tangible and interconnected manner, Maltego offers clarity amid the digital chaos.

Maltego comes pre-installed on Kali; however, if you need to set it up, you can simply use `apt-get` to install it by typing the following:

```
sudo apt-get install maltego
```

Upon the first launch, Maltego will guide you through a setup wizard. This will include creating or logging into a Paterva account, which is essential for accessing certain features and transforms.

Once you've registered and logged in to Maltego, it's time to determine the specific *machine* for your analysis. In the context of Maltego, a **machine** defines the depth and type of footprinting you aim to perform on your target.

Now, in order to get the full benefit of Maltego, you'll need to add in **transforms**, which are basically plugins to third-party services to pull data from. Some transforms are free, and some of the better ones charge for their connections. I'm going to try to keep with just the freebies for this demo.

From the main dashboard, you can filter out all the *pay-to-play* transforms by selecting the **Free (with API key)** option. Here, you can see which transforms I've installed on my Kali system:

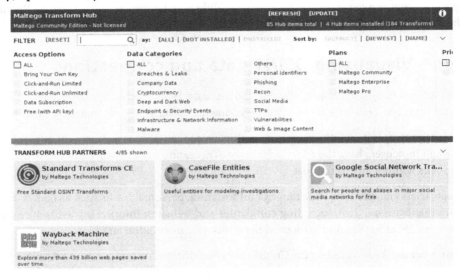

Figure 5.4 – The transforms I've installed on my system

Next, we'll create a new graph by clicking on the **New** icon in the menu bar. Now, we want to add an entity, which is an object that our transforms are providing us. I'm going to scroll down and select a person entity and drag that icon over onto the graph like I'm showing you here:

Figure 5.5 – Here, I've dragged a person entity over onto the graph

You'll notice right away that the default name is John Doe. Now, that's not really who I want to search for, so let's change the name to someone who might be kind of cool to gather intel about. Double-click on the person icon, and let's change it to Elon Musk for giggles. Click **OK**. Now, let's right-click the icon, and you'll see the different transforms you can run:

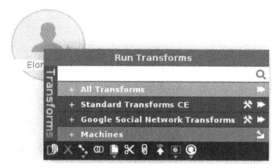

Figure 5.6 – By right-clicking on the object, you can see which transforms you can run

Let's go ahead and run them all and see what happens.

So, we start off seeing several email addresses. Some might be Elon's real email address (such as elon.musk@spacex.com) while others could be someone else or even a spammer's email address). Let's right-click on elon.musk@spacex.com and run all the transforms here:

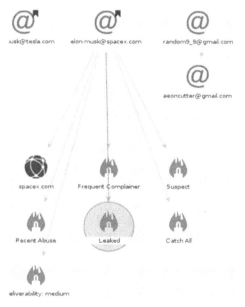

Figure 5.7 – Interesting info after running transforms for elon.musk@spacex.com

If you select the **Leaked** icon, you'll see on the left side that this email address was associated with a database leak:

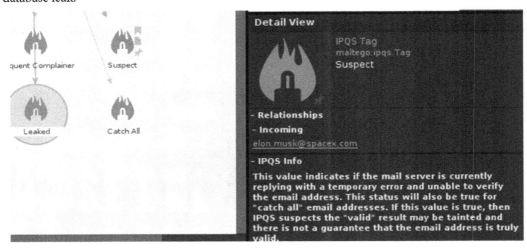

Figure 5.8 – Details about the object show the email was involved in a breach

You can continue to dive deeper into each object that you discover to increase your knowledge of the target. For example, you can run the transforms for the domain of spacex.com, as I did here. You'll notice that so many objects came back that it zoomed out to where all we see are dots that represent additional objects. You can zoom up and navigate around to continue your search for intel:

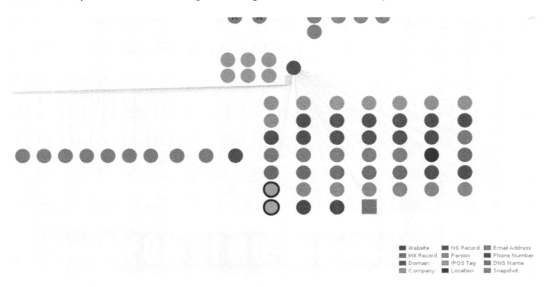

Figure 5.9 – Results for the spacex.com domain

Notice as I zoom in that I'm starting to see other names of people as well as phone numbers starting to appear; this could lead me down another *rabbit hole* of research and investigations:

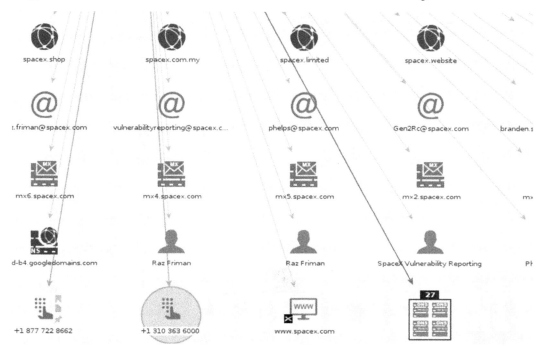

Figure 5.10 – Notice the names and even phone numbers that are populating

Discovering the infrastructure

To start, select a domain and explore the available transforms, which are essentially different functionalities or tasks you can perform. For instance, let's begin with DNS to get some DNS information. We can also look at other transforms to enumerate information such as the mail server and the name service, and find other top-level domains or websites.

First, let's perform a transform to websites, which gives us the website associated with the domain. Next, by right-clicking on the domain icon, we can select the name service, which will provide us with the name service information. From there, we can enumerate subdomains and explore the mail service to understand where the mail is being handled, revealing various mail servers.

Now, let's examine other top-level domains associated with yahoo.com. This process uncovers domains such as yahoo.au, yahoo.email, tokyo, and so on:

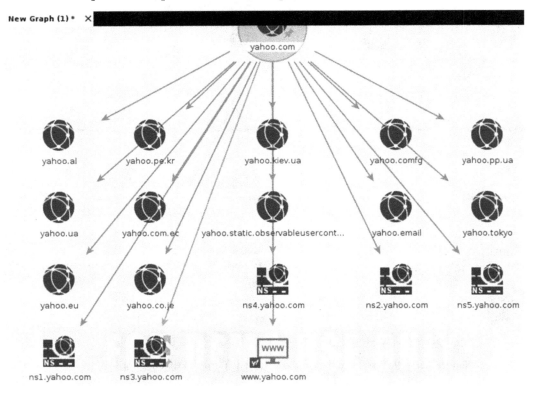

Figure 5.11 – Output of top-level domains, name servers, and websites

The next step is to see if we can resolve some emails. We can try using WHOIS information, PGP, or search engines for this purpose. However, if we don't find any emails from the search engine, that's okay.

Let's see if we can get any IP addresses from the name servers. We can also explore shared websites or domains running on these name servers. By resolving these to various IPs, we can then confirm the owner of these IPs and look for their email addresses, which might come from various sources.

For example, we find emails such as admin@yahooinc.com, which are quite useful. If we resolve these domains, we can group them together and check which name servers they point to, typically the standard Yahoo servers. By grouping all the name servers, we can discover all other domains currently hosted on these servers:

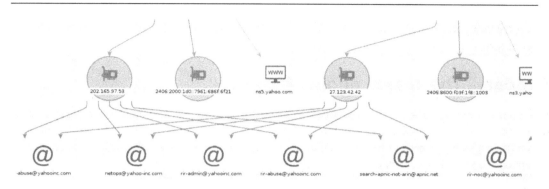

Figure 5.12 – More intel such as emails, IP addresses, and websites

This process might take a while as it runs the transforms, but it eventually provides a comprehensive overview of the structure, including sites such as Yahoo, `yahoologins.com`, `yahoochatrooms`, `rocketmail.ru`, and more:

Figure 5.13 – This is a small overview of yahoo.com's infrastructure

This gives us a good representation of all the information we've gathered and how it relates to each other in terms of domains, name servers, mail servers, and so on. Crazy, huh?

Shodan – The search engine for IoT

Shodan isn't your typical search engine. Instead of searching for websites, Shodan scans the internet for devices. From webcams to traffic lights, if it's connected to the internet, Shodan aims to find it. Given the explosive growth of IoT devices, understanding and leveraging Shodan becomes pivotal for anyone in the cybersecurity and OSINT domain.

While Google helps you find websites, Shodan helps you find devices. It's designed to *see* the internet from a device's perspective. Whether it's a smart fridge, an **Industrial Control System** (**ICS**), or even a city's power grid, if these are improperly secured and connected online, they'll likely show up on Shodan.

Getting started with Shodan

To harness the capabilities of Shodan, do the following:

1. Head to the Shodan website (`https://www.shodan.io/`) and create an account.
2. Once registered, you'll gain access to the search interface. Here, you can input specific terms, IP addresses, or filters to begin your search.
3. A simple search for `webcam` on Shodan can reveal countless cameras connected across the globe. But the real fun begins when you start playing with Shodan's filters. For instance, if you're looking for webcams specifically in Chicago, just type `country: US city:Chicago webcam`, and voilà, you're there.

Shodan's capabilities go beyond just geographical searches. Say you're interested in a pi-hole device. Just type in `dnsmasq-pi-hole" "Recursion: enabled`, and Shodan will show you where these devices are located globally:

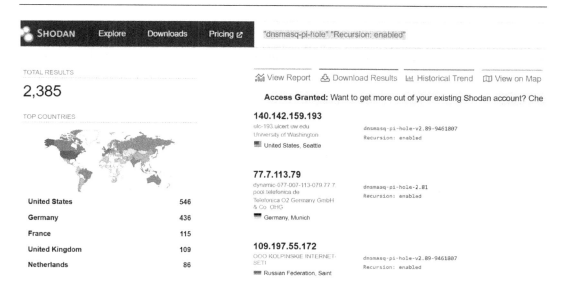

Figure 5.14 – What Shodan found when searching for a pi-hole device

This tool is incredibly useful for security professionals, especially when conducting company security assessments. For example, if you want to see all the devices owned by a company such as Microsoft, just use the org filter with org: Microsoft, and you'll get a comprehensive list.

But what about finding servers running specific services or software? Shodan makes this easy too. If you're looking for servers running SSH (which typically uses port 22), just type port:22 in Shodan. Or, if you're interested in finding servers running a vulnerable version of software, such as Apache version 2.2.15, use the version filter. This feature is particularly useful for identifying potential security risks:

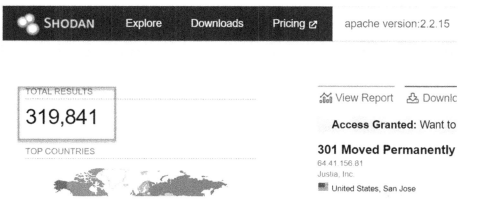

Figure 5.15 – Over 319,000 vulnerable Apache servers still online

Shodan isn't just about finding webcams and servers; it's also a gateway to exploring ICS. By using the `tag:ics` filter, you can delve into the world of industrial controls. And for those concerned about security, Shodan can help find devices that still use default passwords – a common vulnerability in many systems.

One of the more intriguing aspects of Shodan is its ability to expose internet-facing databases. A simple search for `MongoDB`, for instance, can reveal thousands of MongoDB databases accessible online. This is a significant concern from a data security perspective. As ethical security professionals, our goal is to secure these systems, not exploit them. Remember my motto, "*Just because you can doesn't mean you should!*" If you come across an exposed database, it's always a good practice to inform the owner organization about the vulnerability.

Shodan even allows us to monitor real-time data, such as NetWave IP camera feeds, which can be filtered geographically.

If you want more information, you just click on the name of the device in the results, and bam! You are presented with a plethora of intel:

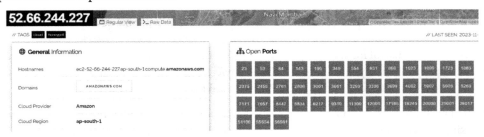

Figure 5.16 – Here, I've clicked on an IP camera to expose more intel

Another remarkable feature of Shodan is its ability to locate smart devices and IoT systems. Using the `iot` search, you can get an overview of connected smart devices in a specific area, highlighting the ubiquity and vulnerability of these devices.

But Shodan's capabilities don't end there. It can even find specific types of errors on web servers, such as those returning a `hacked` header, which is incredibly useful for web developers and system administrators

Shodan also reveals devices you might not typically consider, such as online-accessible printers. This can be crucial for companies looking to prevent confidential information leaks. For cybersecurity enthusiasts, Shodan is a treasure trove of information on server configurations, firewall settings, and security measures, offering a real-time snapshot of the state of internet security.

Using Shodan's API

For those looking to integrate Shodan's capabilities into their applications or automate tasks, Shodan offers an API.

Access your API key from the Shodan dashboard after registration.

This key allows you to automate searches, integrate Shodan into custom tools such as Maltego, or even build new applications harnessing its device-scanning prowess.

Trace Labs – A powerful OS designed just for OSINT

Get ready to immerse yourself in the wonderful world of OSINT with Trace Labs! This brilliant platform is like a funhouse designed just for intel-savvy folks such as us. The moment you log in, you'll see everything is centered on making your investigative life easier. Trace Labs is built on a stripped-down version of Kali Linux, so the interface is extremely familiar. The interface is intuitive and simple to use, letting you focus on searches rather than fumbling with tools. All the essential gear for tracking down details is right at your fingertips, prepped and ready to uncover insights:

Figure 5.17 – Trace Labs desktop

But wait – there's more! This supercharged tool for your utility belt has everything you need to take your online inquiries to the max. The developers really covered all the bases, anticipating the customized workflows of different professionals.

And talk about a supportive community! A team of expert users is there every step of the way to collaborate, give pointers, and make sure you get the most out of the platform. With this all-star crew behind you, you'll be amazed at how quickly your skills improve.

Trace Labs has developed a model to use crowdsourcing to help with missing persons cases that law enforcement has requested public assistance with. They bring together hundreds of skilled investigators through our **Capture The Flag (CTF)** events and ongoing operations to crowdsource any new leads that might be out there on the internet, using only OSINT.

You can download an already prepared virtual machine directly from Trace Labs' website (`https://www.tracelabs.org/initiatives/osint-vm`) and get involved with their initiatives and have access to some cool tools.

Overview of the Aircrack-ng suite

Aircrack-ng is not just a toolbox for testing Wi-Fi security; it's also a powerful tool used in OSINT. This means it helps gather information from publicly available sources, such as Wi-Fi networks, to learn more about them.

In OSINT, finding weak spots in networks is crucial. Aircrack-ng helps identify these weaknesses, showing us which networks might be easy targets for hackers. This way, we can learn about potential risks and how to protect against them.

By observing how these networks operate, Aircrack-ng helps us learn patterns. For example, we can find out when a network is most active or see if any unusual signals stand out.

Aircrack-ng can be used to map out Wi-Fi networks in an area. This is really useful for understanding how networks are spread out in different places, such as in a city or a neighborhood.

For people studying cybersecurity, Aircrack-ng offers a wealth of real-world data. By collecting information from various networks, researchers can understand better how to build stronger and safer Wi-Fi networks.

> **Note**
>
> It's important to remember that while Aircrack-ng can be used to gather lots of information, it should always be used responsibly and ethically. Just as with any powerful tool, it must be used for learning and improving security, not for doing anything harmful or illegal.

When using Aircrack-ng, there are different tools available for specific jobs. Each tool has its own purpose and can be used either alone or with others in the suite to perform wireless network security tasks. The suite includes tools such as the following:

- Airmon-ng enables monitor mode on your wireless adapter to start capturing network traffic
- Airodump-ng captures network traffic and then finds wireless networks and data packets
- Airgraph-ng makes graphical representations of the network traffic

- Aireplay-ng creates network traffic and performs attacks such as deauthentication and packet injection to alter network behavior

- Aircrack-ng is the main tool that cracks **Wired Equivalent Privacy (WEP)** and **Wi-Fi Protected Access (WPA)**/WPA2 encryption keys to assess network security

- Airbase-ng makes fake Wi-Fi **Access Points (APs)** for **Man-in-the-Middle (MitM)** attacks or social engineering attacks

There are also other tools such as `airdecap-ng`, `airdecloak-ng`, and `airtun-ng`, but we won't be focusing on them in this book.

> **Note**
>
> It's important to note the difference between Aircrack-ng (the suite) and `aircrack-ng` (the tool). As of the writing of this text, Kali includes Aircrack-ng, but this may change in the future.

If you need to install Aircrack-ng on either Kali or another Linux distribution, here's the command to do so:

```
sudo apt-get install aircrack-ng
```

Now that we have Aircrack-ng installed, let's jump in.

Airmon-ng

So, what does Airmon-ng do? It's like a switch that turns your Wi-Fi adapter (the thing in your computer that connects to Wi-Fi) into a super listener. Normally, your Wi-Fi adapter just pays attention to the internet stuff meant for your computer. But with Airmon-ng, it starts listening to all Wi-Fi signals around it, even ones not meant for you. This is called **monitor mode**.

Why is monitor mode important? Well, imagine you're a cybersecurity expert or someone who needs to check if a Wi-Fi network is safe. By using Airmon-ng to listen to everything in the air, you can figure out if there are any weak spots in the network or if someone is trying to break in.

Using Airmon-ng is pretty straightforward. First, you need to find out the name of your Wi-Fi adapter (it's usually something such as `wlan0`). You can do this with some simple computer commands. Once you know the name, you use Airmon-ng to switch your adapter into this all-listening mode. Managed mode is the default mode for Wi-Fi adapters, where your adapter only receives packets addressed to your specific MAC address, while monitor mode enables your adapter to receive any packets in range, even if not addressed to your MAC address. Let me show you how we get our Wi-Fi cards into monitor mode:

1. To check the interface name, you can run the following command:

   ```
   ifconfig
   ```

2. Next, you'll want to check to find conflicting processes that could interfere with the interface:

    ```
    sudo airmon-ng
    ```

    Make a note of the interface name as you'll need that here in a second.

3. Next, you'll want to find out if anything is running that will interfere with the Aircrack-ng suite. We do this by typing the following:

    ```
    sudo airmon-ng check
    ```

4. If anything shows up here, you'll want to shut it down by typing the following:

    ```
    sudo airmon-ng check ki
    ```

5. Then, to actively start monitoring and seeing the magic of Wi-Fi, you'll type the following:

    ```
    sudo airmon-ng start <the adaptername you saw above>
    ```

6. Now, type the following:

    ```
    ifconfig
    ```

    You'll see that your adapter has changed its name from wlan0 to wlan0mon:

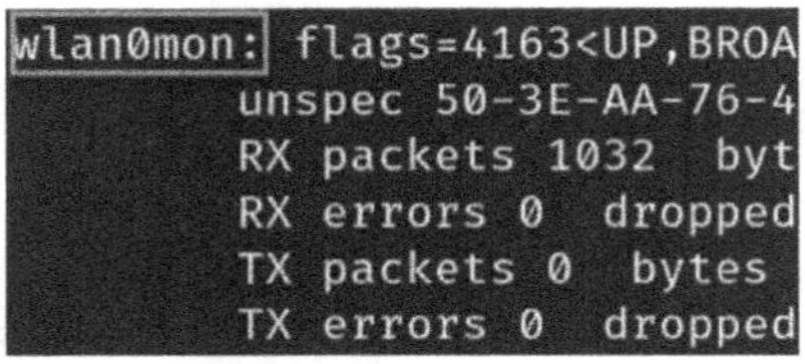

Figure 5.18 – Airmon-ng has changed the name of our adapter

Here, you'll see that in monitor mode, your interface name will change to wlan0won.

In addition to the previously mentioned airmon-ng commands, there are a few more that are helpful. The airmon-ng stop command can be used to disable monitor mode on the interface. Similarly, airmon-ng --channel can be used to set the default channel when enabling monitor mode.

Once we have our **Network Interface Card** (**NIC**) in monitoring mode, we can proceed with capturing the necessary data and performing wireless security checks. This is the first key step that sets the stage for Aircrack-ng.

Airodump-ng

Airodump-ng is another tool in the Aircrack-ng suite, and it's super useful for anyone interested in wireless network security. It's designed to help you gather information about Wi-Fi networks around you.

This is what Airodump-ng does:

- **Captures Wi-Fi data**: Airodump-ng listens to and captures data from Wi-Fi networks. It can see all the Wi-Fi traffic flying around in the air, not just the stuff meant for your device.

- **Sees network details**: It shows you a list of all the Wi-Fi networks it can find, along with important info such as how strong the signal is, what channel they're on, and what kind of security they use.

- **Tracks devices**: Airodump-ng can also see which devices (such as phones or laptops) are connected to each Wi-Fi network.

You run `airodump-ng` after you get `airmon-ng` up and running (that's the process we just showed you how to do in the previous section). You then simply type the following:

```
sudo airodump-ng wlan0mon
```

The output is shown in the following screenshot:

```
CH  5 ][ Elapsed: 12 s ][ 2023-10-20 11:46

BSSID              PWR  Beacons    #Data, #/s  CH   MB    ENC CIPHER   AUTH ESSID

AA:80:88:33:F4:19  -81        4        1    0   5   130   WPA2 CCMP    PSK  MiCasa_2
28:80:88:3B:3B:6F  -81        3        0    0   5   130   WPA2 CCMP    PSK  Mi Casa
92:80:88:3B:3B:60  -75        3        0    0   5   130   WPA2 CCMP    PSK  MiCasa_2
28:80:88:33:F4:18  -81        3        0    0   5   130   WPA2 CCMP    PSK  Mi Casa
80:02:9C:C9:A7:13  -82        4        0    0   1   360   WPA2 CCMP    PSK  GryphonH
80:02:9C:C9:A7:14  -80        6        0    0   1   360   WPA2 CCMP    PSK  GryphonG
9C:A2:F4:16:22:AA  -73       13        9    0   1   130   WPA2 CCMP    PSK  BanburyG
CC:2D:21:B0:47:41  -67       18       11    0   1   130   WPA2 CCMP    PSK  BanburyG
EC:74:27:EF:FB:05  -81        0        0    0  10    -1                     <length:
72:03:9F:04:ED:A4  -53       20        0    0  11    48   WPA2 CCMP    PSK  BatLight
22:E0:19:53:E1:BA  -48       20        0    0  11   360   WPA2 CCMP    PSK  <length:

BSSID              STATION            PWR   Rate    Lost    Frames  Notes  Probes

28:80:88:3B:3B:6F  38:8B:59:9E:C0:7E  -84   0 - 1      0         3
(not associated)   B8:E9:37:F9:6D:97  -64   0 - 1      0         1              Sonos_M
(not associated)   F6:53:E6:36:39:4E  -74   0 - 5     11         2
9C:A2:F4:16:22:AA  D8:07:B6:BF:8B:72  -1   12e- 0      0         1
9C:A2:F4:16:22:AA  10:5A:17:78:0B:4E  -77   0 - 1      0         4
```

Figure 5.19 – Airodump-ng identifying Wi-Fi signals

To narrow down your capturing using `airodump-ng`, there are several common commands you can use. These include the following:

- `--channel`: Select a specific channel to listen on

- `--bssid`: Filter to a specific **Basic Service Set Identifier** (BSSID)

- `-w`: Specify an output file prefix
- `--encrypt`: Filter by encryption type
- `--showack`: Show ACK stats for clients to identify injection vulnerabilities

Here is an example of how to capture using these commands:

```
sudo airodump-ng wlan0mon --channel 6 --bssid <AA:BB:CC:DD:EE:FF> -w
output
```

With `airodump-ng`, you can gather information such as MAC addresses for APs and clients' systems for further analysis and setup for advanced attacks with Aircrack-ng.

Aireplay-ng

Deauthentication attacks, executed through Aireplay-ng, form a critical component in the arsenal of network security testing. These attacks disrupt the wireless communication between a client and the AP, forcibly disconnecting them. The technique leverages deauthentication packets, which are part of the Wi-Fi protocol but are exploited to sever connections. This process is instrumental in testing network resilience against **Denial-of-Service** (**DoS**) attacks and in facilitating the capture of WPA/WPA2 handshakes.

To use `aireplay-ng`, you need to provide the following information:

- The type of attack, using `-deauth` as an example
- The target network, using the `-a` switch along with the BSSID of the target
- You should also provide the monitoring interface, such as `wlan0mon`, as well as the MAC addresses of the target AP/client

Here's an example of what a command would look like with `aireplay-ng`:

```
sudo aireplay-ng --deauth 100 -a <AA:BB:CC:DD:EE:FF> -c
<11:22:33:44:55:66> wlan0mon
```

Some common `aireplay-ng` commands are the following:

- `--deauth`: This is used for deauthentication attacks
- `--fakeauth`: This command is used for fake authentication attacks
- `--arpreplay`: This command is used for **Address Resolution Protocol** (**ARP**) request replay attacks
- `-a`: This is used to specify the target AP BSSID
- `-c`: This is used to specify the target client's MAC address

Aireplay-ng's capabilities extend to a broad spectrum of testing scenarios. By simulating various attack vectors, from basic deauthentication to complex ARP injections, it provides an in-depth analysis of a network's security. This tool is instrumental in identifying weaknesses, testing network response to hostile activities, and validating the effectiveness of security measures in place.

Aircrack-ng

Aircrack-ng is crucial for testing network security by breaking encryption keys. It's important to know how to crack WEP and WPA/WPA2 encryptions. WEP, being older and less secure, is easier to crack due to its weaknesses. WPA and WPA2 are tougher, but they can still be cracked, especially with weak passwords, using more advanced techniques.

To crack WPA/WPA2, Aircrack-ng mainly uses two methods: dictionary and brute-force attacks. Dictionary attacks try passwords from a pre-made list, while brute-force attacks test all character combinations until the right one is found. The success of these methods depends on the password's strength and the wordlist's quality.

In addition to dictionary and brute-force attacks, when cracking WPA/WPA2 with Aircrack-ng, using a `.cap` file is crucial. This file contains captured data packets from the network. By analyzing these packets, particularly the ones involved in the handshake process, Aircrack-ng attempts to decrypt the network key. The success of cracking the password depends on the information captured in the `.cap` file, which includes the handshake data necessary for deciphering the network's encryption key.

Some common `aircrack-ng` commands include the following:

- `-w`: To specify the wordlist or dictionary file
- `-b`: To specify the target AP BSSID
- `-e`: To specify the target network **Extended SSID (ESSID)**
- `-a`: To specify the attack mode (2 for WPA/**WPA2-Pre-Shared Key (WPA2 PSK)**

To crack hidden WPA/WPA2-PSK networks, you need to tag the ESSID with `-e` like this:

```
sudo aircrack-ng -w dictionary.txt -b <AA:BB:CC:DD:E:FF> output-01.cap
```

After finding a possible key, Aircrack-ng checks if it can decrypt the network's data. This is crucial to see how strong the encryption is and to identify weak spots. It also helps understand what kinds of passwords are easier to crack, which is useful for creating stronger password policies.

Airbase-ng

Airbase-ng is another cool tool that is a part of the Aircrack-ng suite. It allows you to create fake APs. Setting up pretend Wi-Fi spots with Airbase-ng is like laying a clever trap to see how tough our networks are and if people can spot the trick. Picture Airbase-ng as a toolbox in the Aircrack-ng kit, letting tech pros build these decoy Wi-Fi spots. It's like putting up a stage and seeing how gadgets and folks react, teaching us heaps about keeping our Wi-Fi safe and sound.

Creating these fake spots is pretty simple. You just pick a channel and a Wi-Fi name (that's the ESSID) that looks legit. Then, you decide if you want this mock Wi-Fi to ask for a password or not. It's all about making it look real.

But there's more! These fake Wi-Fi spots aren't just for show. They're the starting point for something called MitM attacks. It's a sneaky move where a hacker secretly messes with messages between people who think they're talking directly to each other. By setting up a fake Wi-Fi, the hacker gets in the middle, listens in, or even changes the data.

Setting up a fake AP with `airbase-ng` requires specific details. You choose an ESSID (the Wi-Fi name), a channel, and whether it's encrypted or not. You also need to set your computer to monitor Wi-Fi traffic using the `wlan0mon` interface that you created with `airmon-ng`. Then, you tweak your settings so that your fake Wi-Fi looks just like the real deal, using a command like this:

```
sudo airbase-ng -a <AA:BB:CC:DD:EE:FF> --essid <FakeAPName> --channel
<#> wlan0mon
```

Here are some common `airbase-ng` commands that you can use to customize your fake AP:

- `-a`: Sets the fake AP BSSID
- `--essid`: Sets the fake AP ESSID
- `--channel`: Sets the channel
- `-W 1`: Enables WEP
- `-z`: Enables WPA/WPA2

With `airbase-ng`'s flexibility and range of options, it becomes a valuable tool in Aircrack-ng for anyone looking to test network security.

Airgraph-ng

Airgraph-ng is a key part of the Aircrack-ng suite that helps you understand your wireless network better. It turns complex network data into graphs that are easy to read. These graphs show a lot of important things about your network, such as how much data is moving through it, which devices are connected, and possible security issues.

The first step in using Airgraph-ng is to collect network data with Airodump-ng. This data is what you'll use to create your graphs. Using `airgraph-ng` requires an input CSV file from `airodump-ng` and specifying an output file for the graph. For example, if want a **Client to AP Relationship (CAPR)** graph that would show you connections and data packets, you'd use this command:

```
sudo airgraph-ng -i output-01.csv -o output.png -g CAPR
```

Some common `airgraph-ng` commands to gather more intel include the following:

- `-i`: Input CSV file
- `-o`: Output graph file
- `-g`: Graph type
- `-c`: Channel filter
- `--essid`: Filter by ESSID

The graphs you make with Airgraph-ng are helpful for understanding your network. They take complex data and make it simpler to see patterns and spot problems. For example, you can see if there's a lot of data moving at certain times or if there are devices on your network that shouldn't be there. These graphs are especially useful for finding unusual activities that could be security threats.

Finding hidden networks

Understanding the basics of Aircrack-ng is a crucial step in uncovering hidden networks. It is important to realize that although a network may be hidden, it is not completely invisible. It is similar to a bad magician at a children's party who pretends to make something disappear but can be easily spotted by a careful observer. Likewise, the name or SSID of a hidden network is not openly broadcasted, but with the right tools, we can reveal what is trying to stay concealed. So, it is important to remember that finding a hidden network is not impossible, and with the right approach, it can be easily achieved.

First things first, you'll want to switch your wireless card into monitor mode so that it will show you all the secret Wi-Fi signals flying through the air:

```
airmon-ng start wlan0
```

You are now all set to begin monitoring all networks in close proximity with this command:

```
airodump-ng wlan0mon
```

In the list that pops up, hidden networks will show the SSID as just `<length: x>`. But here's where the magic happens – anyone connected to that hidden network is constantly shouting out probe requests asking to reconnect. And these requests conveniently reveal the hidden SSID every time!

```
 CH  9 ][ BAT: 3 hours 9 mins ][ Elapsed: 8 s ][ 2012-05-20 11:10

 BSSID              PWR  Beacons    #Data, #/s  CH  MB   ENC  CIPHER AUTH ESSID
 28:EF:01:34:64:91  -29      19         1    0   6  54e  WPA2 CCMP   PSK  Linksys
 28:EF:01:35:34:85  -42      17         0    0   6  54e  WPA2 CCMP   PSK  <length:6:

 BSSID              STATION          PWR   Rate    Lost  Packets  Probes
 28:EF:01:35:34:85  28:EF:01:23:46:68  -57   0 - 1     0        1
```

Figure 5.20 – Notice that airodump-ng identifies this AP's ESSID as <length:6:>

So, we just have to force a connected device to send out a probe request by briefly disconnecting it with the following command:

```
aireplay-ng -0 30 -a [AP MAC] -c [Client MAC] wlan0mon
```

The -0 flag sends the disconnect signal, and 30 identifies the number of packets to send.

Once we deauth the client, switch back over to airodump-ng, and you'll see the hidden SSID magically appear! Easy peasy lemon squeezy:

```
28:EF:01:35:34:85   -42          17          0    0    6  54e  WPA2 CCMP   PSK  SkyNet

BSSID               STATION              PWR   Rate   Lost  Packets  Probes
28:EF:01:35:34:85   28:EF:01:23:46:68    -57   0 - 1     0        1  SkyNet
```

Figure 5.21 – Airodump-ng reveals the SSID as SkyNet

While hiding your SSID seems sneaky, it's child's play for a hacker to uncover. Don't let it give you a false sense of security! Be sure to use strong encryption, passwords, and other protections as well.

Speaking of deauth attacks, we can use these to create MitM attacks, which can lead to data interception. This can be a serious issue that needs to be addressed.

Firstly, a hacker sends deauth messages to force you off the real Wi-Fi network. This can be really frustrating!

The next step involves the hacker setting up a router with the same network name as the real one (we call this an Evil Twin). Your device, thinking it has reconnected to the real network, has actually connected to the fake one.

Now comes the *MitM* part – any data you send on the fake network gets intercepted by the hacker. This includes sensitive information such as passwords, messages, and emails. It's a scary thought, isn't it?

Additional open source OSINT tools

OSINT tools span a broad spectrum, offering capabilities that range from domain information extraction to social media monitoring. These tools, accessible to anyone, can often be modified to suit specific needs due to their open source nature. Next is a selection of standout open source OSINT tools, their features, and their utilization within Kali Linux.

SpiderFoot

SpiderFoot is an incredibly powerful OSINT automation tool that integrates various data sources to gather and centralize information about a specific target. This can be an IP address, domain name, email address, or even a username. With more than 200 modules, SpiderFoot consolidates a broad swath of digital intelligence, making it easier for investigators to analyze and interpret.

To install SpiderFoot, you would open a Terminal and type the following:

```
sudo apt install spiderfoot
```

SpiderFoot can be started by executing sf.py from its directory, but ensure Python 3 is being used. Many Linux distributions default to 2.7:

```
python3 sf.py -l 127.0.0.1:5001
```

The output is shown in the following screenshot:

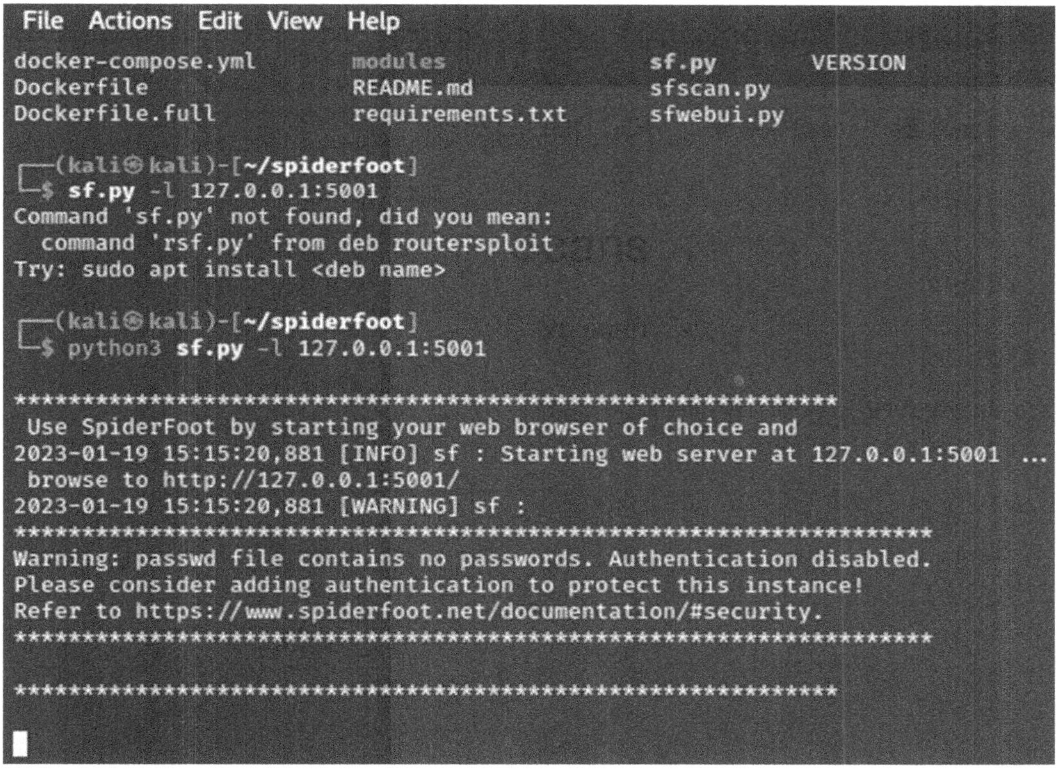

Figure 5.22 – Starting up SpiderFoot using the sf.py command

After starting the SpiderFoot service, open a browser and enter the following URL:

```
127.0.0.1:5001
```

You should see a web interface like the one shown next. Let's click the **New Scan** tab and fill out the information that is needed to identify the target. I'll use `hackthissite.org` in this example:

Figure 5.23 – Configuring a new scan in SpiderFoot

Click on the **Run Scan Now** button and wait for the scan to complete. It may take some time, but eventually, you will be able to see a lot of information about the site. Please note that my favorite word – *plethora* – might be used to describe the amount of intel you'll receive:

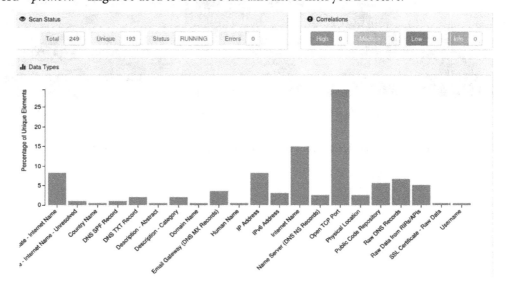

Figure 5.24 – Output from SpiderFoot

SpiderFoot has a really cool feature where you can zoom in on any column to get more information. This means you can easily explore and analyze the data in greater detail. Simply click on any column that catches your attention, and the tool will automatically zoom in and display all the relevant information. It's a powerful and user-friendly feature that makes analyzing data a breeze!

Twint

Twint stands for **Twitter Intelligence Tool**. It's an advanced X, formerly Twitter scraping tool that allows for the extraction of tweets from Twitter profiles without using Twitter's API. This is a significant advantage because it bypasses the limitations imposed by the Twitter API, such as rate limits and the inability to access older tweets.

Some of its key features include no Twitter API required, which collects a wide range of data from tweets, including date, time, and content, as well as information about likes and retweets, and gathers data from Twitter user profiles, including followers, followings, number of tweets, and location information.

You can add Twint to your Kali or Trace Labs OS by opening a Terminal and typing each of the following commands:

```
git clone --depth=1 https://github.com/twintproject/twint.git
cd twint
pip3 install . -r requirements.txt
pip3 install twint
```

The main command for fetching tweets is shown here:

```
twint -u username
```

This collects all tweets from a user's timeline. To search tweets for a keyword, use the following:

```
twint -u username -s batman
```

The -s flag looks for batman in the target user's tweets. You can also search all tweets globally:

```
twint -s batman
```

Here are some other examples:

```
twint -u username --year 2023 # Tweets before 2023
twint -u username --since 2020-12-20 # Tweets after Dec 20, 2020
twint -u username -o tweets.csv --csv # Save Tweets to a CSV
```

Here's the command to get a user's profile info:

```
twint -u username --user-full
```

To gather a user's followers or follows, use these commands:

```
twint -u username --followers
twint -u username --following
```

Here are the commands for fetching full user details on connections:

```
twint -u username --followers --user-full
twint -u username --following --user-full
```

You can also save tweets in various formats:

```
twint -u username -o tweets.json --json
twint -u username -o tweets.db --database
twint -u username -o file.txt
```

You can also output to Elasticsearch and SQLite. And if you import Twint as a module, you can fully customize the output.

As you can see, Twint gives you access to the tweets and metadata Twitter keeps locked down. Learn its query language, and an ocean of vital Twitter data is at your fingertips.

Some final thoughts on tools

I know we've talked about lots of tools up to now, but the one thing that makes the hair on the back of my neck stand up is the amount of intel we expose unwittingly, either through social media or by registering for apps or any online service. Our information is everywhere. This intel can be easily accessed without tools, but rather just using some deduction skills and command sense.

One of the most prominent TikTok investigators is Shay, known as @shay.nanigans87. With over 360,000 followers as of November 2023, Shay has garnered fame for her ability to track down strangers on the internet using only the smallest clues. Her videos show her zooming in on tiny details in photos, deciphering blurred-out details, and piecing together information to identify random people who've challenged her to find them:

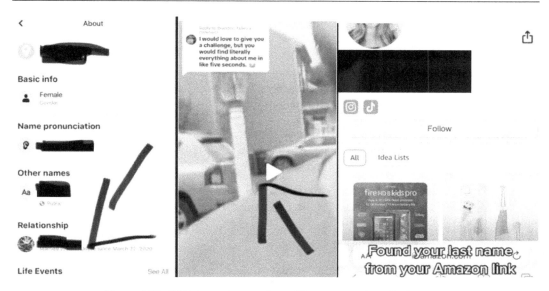

Figure 5.25 – TikToker @shay.nanigans87 uses no tools to find targets

In one video, Shay demonstrates how she can take a partial shipping label from a box in someone's photo and figure out their address. In another, she enhances a blurry store receipt to read the purchaser's name. Her videos are a captivating display of digital detective work.

While Shay maintains she only uses her abilities ethically, her videos serve as a reminder that our privacy may be more fragile than we realize in the digital age.

Another question after playing with all these tools is: How do you keep up with OSINT tools and techniques? Well, let's talk about that next.

Keeping up with the open source OSINT landscape

As technology progresses, the tools and techniques used in the field adapt to stay relevant and effective. Whether it's the introduction of new platforms or the emergence of cutting-edge tools, staying updated with the latest developments is crucial for OSINT professionals.

Blogs and websites

Many cybersecurity researchers, intelligence professionals, and hobbyists maintain blogs and websites where they discuss the latest OSINT techniques, tools, and case studies. Regularly reading these can provide insights into the newest trends and best practices. Websites such as *Bellingcat*, *OSINT Essentials*, and *OSINT Techniques* are gold mines of information:

- **Bellingcat** (`https://www.bellingcat.com/`): An investigative journalism website that specializes in fact-checking and OSINT. They often publish detailed methodologies behind their investigations, which serve as excellent learning material.

- **OSINT Curious** (`https://www.osintcurio.us/`): A project focused on OSINT news and resources. They offer webcasts, blogs, tools, and tips for the OSINT community.

- **Sector035's Week in OSINT** (`https://sector035.nl/`): A weekly roundup of interesting links and news around the OSINT community.

- **IntelTechniques** (`https://inteltechniques.com/`): Maintained by Michael Bazzell, a former FBI cybercrime investigator. The website provides a plethora of tools, training, and resources related to OSINT.

- **OSINT Essentials** (`https://www.osintessentials.com/`): A resource-rich site that provides numerous tools, references, and guides for OSINT professionals and enthusiasts.

- **OSINT Techniques** (`https://www.osinttechniques.com/`): A handy resource site with categorized OSINT tools and instructional content.

Conferences and workshops

Every year, big cybersecurity conferences such as *DEF CON*, *Black Hat*, and *Bsides* have special sessions on OSINT. These events are great for learning about OSINT by actually doing it. The instructors are often some of the best in this area. Plus, these conferences are a great place to meet other people who work in cybersecurity, which can help you learn more and grow in your career.

Evaluating new tools

When checking out new OSINT tools, you should think about a few important things to make sure they're good for you:

- **Who made it**: Check who created the tool. Look up the name of the developer or company online to see if they are known and trusted in the OSINT community.

- **How it helps you**: Ask yourself questions such as: Does this tool do something that I can't do with my current tools? Is it faster or more accurate? If it just does the same things as your other tools, it might not be worth using.

- **What other users say**: Look for reviews or comments from people who have used the tool. You can find these on online forums, social media, or websites that talk about OSINT tools. Pay attention to what they say about how easy the tool is to use, how well it works, and if they have had any problems with it.

- **Updates and improvements**: Good tools are updated regularly by their creators. This means they get better over time, fix any problems, and adapt to new challenges in OSINT work. Check the tool's website or online forums to see how often it gets updated and if the updates really improve it.

By thinking about these things, you can pick the best OSINT tools that are safe and useful and keep up with the latest changes in the world of cybersecurity.

Engaging with the OSINT community

The OSINT community is vast and diverse, with professionals from various backgrounds and expertise levels. Engaging with this community can provide the following benefits:

- **Collaborative learning**: Sharing experiences, challenges, and solutions can lead to collective growth.

- **New perspectives**: Different individuals might approach a problem differently. Engaging with others can provide fresh viewpoints and techniques.

- **Networking**: Building relationships within the community can open up opportunities for collaboration, mentorship, and even job prospects.

Summary

In this chapter, we looked at some really useful OSINT tools such as Recon-ng, Maltego, Shodan, and Tracelabs-OS. Each of these tools helps us in different ways to understand and use OSINT better. For example, Maltego helps us see how different pieces of data are connected, and Shodan lets us explore IoT. We also talked about other tools such as Aircrack-ng, SpiderFoot, and Twint, and how important it is to keep learning and sharing in the OSINT community.

Next up, we'll learn how smart uses of OSINT can help spot and stop cyber risks, keeping both people and companies safe online.

Get this book's PDF version and more

Scan the QR code (or go to packtpub.com/unlock). Search for this book by name, confirm the edition, and then follow the steps on the page.

UNLOCK NOW

Note: Keep your invoice handy. Purchases made directly from Packt don't require an invoice.

The Eyes and Ears of Threat Intelligence – How OSINT Helps Mitigate Cyber Risks

This chapter marks a turning point – the moment we transition from **Open Source Intelligence** (**OSINT**) theory into real-world cybersecurity application. The time has come to take our foundational knowledge and harness it practically to supercharge threat intelligence efforts.

In this chapter, we'll cover the following aspects:

- Introduction to threat intelligence and OSINT
- Cyber threats and OSINT
- Cyber threat intelligence platforms and OSINT integration
- Building an OSINT-driven threat intelligence program
- Case study: OSINT in a real-world cybersecurity incident

By the end of this chapter, you will be proficient in OSINT. You will understand its importance in identifying potential threats using a combination of wisdom, digital expertise, and perception. Moreover, you will be equipped to apply these skills strategically to any aspect of cybersecurity that involves human interaction – which is nearly everywhere in today's world. It's time to put theory into practice – let's get started!

Introduction to threat intelligence and OSINT

First off, let's talk about why OSINT is such a big deal in cyber threat intelligence. In the digital world, information is power, and OSINT provides a wealth of information from publicly available sources. Whether it's social media, online forums, websites, or databases, OSINT taps into these resources to give us insights that could easily be overlooked. This is crucial because it helps us to get ahead of threats, sometimes even before they fully materialize.

But how exactly is OSINT used in the realm of cyber threats? It's all about gathering pieces of the digital puzzle and putting them together. For instance, OSINT can help in identifying potential vulnerabilities in software and systems that hackers might exploit. It can also be used to track the digital footprints of cybercriminals and understand their tactics and patterns. This kind of intelligence is invaluable in not just reacting to threats but proactively preparing for them.

One of the most exciting aspects of OSINT is how it complements other forms of intelligence such as **Human Intelligence (HUMINT)** and **Signal Intelligence (SIGINT)**. HUMINT is about understanding threats by talking to people and watching what they do, which gives us deep insight into why attacks happen. SIGINT is about listening in on communications, such as emails, to get detailed info on threats.

When we use all three together, we get a full view of cyber threats, helping us to predict, stop, and react to cyber problems better.

Now, let's not forget about the challenges. Integrating OSINT into cyber threat intelligence isn't just about collecting information; it's about analyzing it effectively. The sheer volume of data can be overwhelming, and not all of it is relevant or accurate. This is where skilled analysts come in, using their expertise to sift through the noise and extract actionable intelligence. It's a skill that requires continuous learning and adaptation, especially as the digital landscape and threat tactics evolve.

Cyber threats and OSINT

New cyber threats constantly emerge to challenge our virtual defenses. Hackers and cybercriminals have proven themselves creative shapeshifters, always searching for new vulnerabilities to exploit for profit and disruption. Cyber threats stay sneaky to cause trouble in our online world. Global events such as big political conflicts also shake things up online. Hackers use this chaos to cause more confusion and carry out their malicious activities. And, get this: cybercriminals are getting smarter at tricking security measures, such as the extra login codes you receive.

But wait, there's more! The stealing of private information, from personal details to company secrets, is on the rise. It's like having a digital pickpocket take your data without you even noticing. As soon as new cyber defenses go up, these shape-shifting threats find clever new ways to sneak past. We've got to stay agile and keep each other alert to how they might strike next. It's an ongoing battle to protect our digital spaces. Phishing and social engineering are some of the most dangerous threats that organizations face. Unlike technical flaws, these threats exploit human vulnerabilities, which makes them harder to detect and prevent. OSINT offers powerful tools and techniques to identify and analyze these threats more effectively, making it an invaluable resource for organizations looking to stay ahead of cybercriminals.

OSINT is also becoming a superhero in the fight against fake news. With so much misinformation floating around, OSINT tools help separate fact from fiction.

Most recently one notable event where OSINT tools were used to debunk fake news involved a video of Ukrainian President Volodymyr Zelensky. In this incident, a deepfake video was released depicting Zelensky declaring an end to the conflict with Russia and surrendering. This video was later identified as fake. Analytical techniques focusing on inconsistencies in lighting, shadows, and movements in the video helped disprove its authenticity. And with more people becoming aware of cybersecurity, there's a growing demand for OSINT tools to help keep everyone safe online.

Phishing

Imagine this: You're casually browsing your email and come across one that looks like it's from a well-known company, say, your bank. It asks you to click on a link and update some personal information. Without a second thought, you might just click and enter your details, right? But wait – this is how phishing scams trick you! These scams are a big headache because they can lead to your sensitive information being leaked or, worse, downloading malicious software onto your computer.

Now, here's where the plot thickens. These cunning phishing campaigns don't just vanish without a trace. They often leave digital footprints scattered across the internet. This is where you'd use your OSINT training to step in. You'd want to look out for things such as fake websites that look eerily similar to real ones, or they might analyze email patterns to catch signs of impersonation (that's called **spoofing**). Plus, they keep an eye on places like forums or even the dark web for any leaked data that might signal an ongoing phishing scheme.

Let's talk about a handy tool in the OSINT toolkit: theHarvester. Remember when we mentioned it back in *Chapter 2*? It's like a Swiss Army knife for gathering online intel. With theHarvester, security analysts can find a treasure trove of information – emails, subdomains, employee names, and even open ports – from public sources such as search engines and social media. For example, using a command such as `theHarvester -d packtpub.com -b all` helps extract all sorts of data about a specific domain. This is super useful in sniffing out potential phishing traps. Think of a bogus website that's a carbon copy of a legitimate business, set up just to swipe user credentials.

Figure 6.1 – theHarvester searching the packtpub.com domain

Here's a twist, though. In real-life scenarios, especially in big organizations, once a phishing campaign is exposed, the fake domain used is usually taken down pronto. It's like playing a game of Whack-A-Mole – as soon as one is hit, it disappears. That's why it's so important for cybersecurity teams to act fast, using tools such as theHarvester, to track down these phishing attempts before they vanish into thin air.

Social engineering

Social engineering is a complex and ever-evolving threat in the cyber world. It's not just about stealing an IP address; it involves a wide range of tactics, from manipulating usernames and email IDs, to exploiting connected devices such as home webcams. The depth and breadth of these attacks are staggering, and they often blend into our digital lives so seamlessly that we might not even notice them.

Understanding the landscape

To get a handle on social engineering, cybersecurity experts use OSINT to unravel what attackers have learned. Here, attackers sometimes get careless. They might leave clues or even brag about their exploits. That's why smart analysts keep an eye on these spaces, monitoring specific keywords, hashtags, or topics linked to phishing and social engineering. For instance, a sudden spike in complaints about fishy emails on a social platform could hint at an ongoing attack.

Tools of the trade

One powerful ally in this battle is **SpiderFoot**. It's like a digital detective that can automate the search for information across numerous sources. By inputting a command such as `spiderfoot -l 127.0.0.1:5001 -s packtpub.com`, an analyst can kickstart a comprehensive scan. This scan can reveal a goldmine of data – email addresses, domain names, and social media profiles – all of which could be exploited in a social engineering attack.

However, social engineering isn't just about what's visible; it's also about uncovering the hidden. This is where tools such as Maltego come into play. Maltego excels at digging deeper, revealing connections between people, companies, and internet infrastructure that might not be immediately apparent.

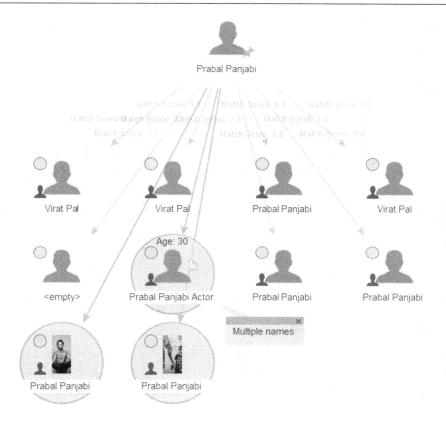

Figure 6.2 – Maltego showing social connections that might not be blatantly available

For example, it can trace the digital footprint of a seemingly innocuous email address to discover connected devices, possibly even a home webcam that's been unknowingly hijacked.

Bridging gaps with OSINT

It's not just about active threats; sometimes the danger lies in social engineering attacks that have already happened. Sites such as *Have I Been Pwned* serve as early warning systems, allowing individuals to check if their data has been compromised. But this is just the tip of the iceberg. The true scope of social engineering encompasses much more – orphaned sites, unsecured webcams, network devices, and even firewalls that are still online are all potential entry points for attackers.

Another aspect of OSINT research in this context is the analysis of leaked data and breach reports. Sites such as *Have I Been Pwned* (`https://haveibeenpwned.com/`) allow users to check if their data has been part of a known breach. This information is crucial, as compromised data often becomes the foundation for social engineering attacks.

Social media platforms are goldmines for attackers. They scour these platforms for personal details to build trust or impersonate individuals in spear-phishing campaigns. OSINT techniques in this context involve meticulous monitoring of posts, connections, and activity patterns to spot potential vulnerabilities.

The bigger picture

By methodically applying these OSINT methods, cybersecurity experts can peel back the layers of social engineers' strategies. They can understand not just the *how* but also the *who* and *why* behind these attacks. This insight is crucial for developing robust defenses, such as awareness campaigns that address common phishing tactics or enhanced security protocols for frequently targeted sectors.

Through comprehensive analysis, we can identify the types of organizations that are at risk, the geographical areas that are most targeted, and the sophistication of the methods used. This is the kind of intelligence that turns the tables on social engineers, transforming potential victims into informed, prepared defenders.

Malware and ransomware

Malware and ransomware have become increasingly sophisticated and damaging, with ransomware, in particular, seeing a dramatic rise and causing widespread disruption:

- **Malware evolution**: Initially simple viruses or worms, malware has evolved into more complex forms, including spyware, Trojans, and keyloggers. These are designed to steal data, disrupt operations, or gain unauthorized system access.

- **Ransomware trends**: Modern ransomware attacks involve encrypting a victim's data and demanding a ransom for the decryption key. These attacks have targeted individuals, businesses, and even government agencies, with the ransom demands often payable in cryptocurrencies.

OSINT in combating malware and ransomware

Analyzing malware and ransomware can be quite relevant in the field of OSINT. Here's how:

- **Understanding threat actors**: Malware and ransomware are often developed and deployed by threat actors, which can range from individual hackers to organized crime syndicates and state-sponsored groups. By analyzing these malicious pieces of software, OSINT specialists can gather insights into the **Tactics, Techniques, and Procedures** (**TTPs**) of these actors. This can include understanding their targets and methods of attack, and even potentially identifying their origin or affiliations.

- **Cybersecurity trends**: Analysis of malware and ransomware contributes to a broader understanding of current cybersecurity threats and trends. This is valuable in OSINT to predict future attacks, understand the evolution of cyber threats, and stay ahead in intelligence gathering.

- **Digital footprints**: Malware and ransomware often leave digital footprints that can be traced back. Analyzing these can lead to uncovering domains, IP addresses, and other digital indicators associated with the attackers. This information can be cross-referenced with open source databases and tools to expand the understanding of the threat landscape.

- **Threat intelligence sharing**: The insights gained from analyzing malware and ransomware can be valuable for threat intelligence sharing within the cybersecurity community. This collaborative approach can help in fortifying defenses against these threats and contribute to a larger pool of OSINT.

- **Countermeasures and mitigation**: Understanding the specifics of how different types of malware and ransomware operate allows for the development of more effective countermeasures and mitigation strategies. This is crucial for organizations looking to protect their assets and can be a key aspect of OSINT-driven cybersecurity strategies.

OSINT tools such as VirusTotal allow for the analysis of malware samples, providing insights into their behavior, origin, and potential impact.

By monitoring IP addresses and domain registrations, cybersecurity professionals can track the infrastructure used by malware and ransomware campaigns. In fact, let's say you come across a website, say `packtpub.com`, and you're unsure about its safety. With VirusTotal, you could enter the URL `https://packtpub.com` and check its credibility.

Figure 6.3 – Packtpub.com scanned by VirusTotal.com

The URL is scanned against VirusTotal's database of known threats. The scan results can reveal whether the site is associated with any malicious activities, such as distributing malware or being part of a phishing campaign. This immediate assessment helps users avoid potentially harmful websites and alerts cybersecurity teams to take necessary actions if a threat is detected.

Now I know that was a lot to take in, so let's try looking at an example. Imagine you've noticed unusual activity suggesting a malware attack on a network you're monitoring. To investigate, you decide to use an OSINT tool such as VirusTotal for a practical demonstration:

1. **Collect suspicious files or URLs**: First, you gather the suspicious files or URLs from the network traffic. These might be files downloaded by users or links they were tricked into clicking.

2. **Analysis with VirusTotal**: You upload these files or enter the URLs into VirusTotal. This tool scans the files or web pages against databases of known malware signatures and behaviors.

3. **Review the report**: VirusTotal provides a detailed report for each file or URL, highlighting any malicious behaviors, connections to known malware families, or communication with suspicious IP addresses.

4. **Cross-reference information**: With the information from VirusTotal, you cross-reference the **Indicators of Compromise (IoCs)** such as IP addresses, domain names, or file hashes with other OSINT databases. This helps you understand whether these indicators are part of larger, known threat campaigns.

5. **Take action**: Based on your findings, you update your network's security measures. This could include blocking malicious IPs, applying patches to prevent exploitation, or educating users about the threat.

6. **Share findings**: Lastly, you prepare a brief on your investigation, highlighting how you used OSINT tools to uncover and mitigate the malware threat. This is shared with the cybersecurity community to aid in collective defense efforts.

Looking at network traffic to catch malware

Analyzing network traffic is a great way to catch malware and ransomware before it causes harm. By looking closely at data flowing in and out of a network, analysts can spot weird activity that shows a system is infected. For example, if there is suddenly a spike in data sent out to a strange website, it could mean botnet or theft activity. Using packet inspector tools such as Wireshark (`https://www.wireshark.org/`) allows continuous and detailed monitoring of network actions. Any odd connections, protocols, or payloads should be checked out.

With network monitoring, issues can often be contained quickly before spreading more. But no single organization sees the whole internet. This is where collaborative platforms such as VirusTotal help out a lot. By letting security researchers upload malware samples and scan suspicious files, new threats can be flagged quickly and signatures shared globally. Crowd-sourced databases such as VirusTotal and ThreatCrowd (`http://ci-www.threatcrowd.org/`) make an early alert system for new attacks.

Figure 6.4 – Threatcrowd.org can provide insight into your IP, domain, or email address

Combining network monitoring and community threat intelligence gives organizations the best shot at staying ahead of ransomware and cyber threats. Being proactive means both watching your own systems closely and coordinating with partners across the industry.

Threat intelligence feeds

Think of threat intelligence feeds as like your social media newsfeed, but instead of pictures and status updates, they're filled with the latest news about cyber threats. These feeds gather information from lots of different places on the internet – such as security forums, hacker sites, and even tweets from cybersecurity experts. They give us real-time updates about new types of malware and ransomware:

*   Why are they important?

    Having this information is super important for people working to protect computers and data from hackers. Just like a weather app warns you about a storm coming, these feeds warn cybersecurity teams about digital storms brewing in the form of cyber attacks.

- How do they help?

  - **Early warnings**: These feeds can alert us about a new virus spreading or if there's a sudden increase in hacking attempts. This is like getting a heads-up before the problem reaches us, giving us time to prepare and protect our systems.

  - **Trend analysis**: By looking at the patterns in these feeds, experts can figure out what types of attacks are becoming more common. This helps in predicting and preparing for what might happen next in the cyber world.

Imagine your cybersecurity team is monitoring AlienVault OTX to stay ahead of cyber threats. One day, they notice an alert about a new ransomware variant spreading through email phishing campaigns. The feed provides detailed IoCs, such as malicious IP addresses, email subjects, and file hashes associated with the ransomware.

Armed with this information, the team quickly updates their email filters to block emails matching the suspicious subjects and indicators. They also configure their security systems to detect and isolate communication with the reported malicious IPs. By acting on the real-time intelligence from AlienVault OTX, they prevent the ransomware from breaching their network, showcasing the critical role these feeds play in proactive cybersecurity defense.

APTs

Advanced Persistent Threats (APTs) represent one of the most insidious forms of cyber threats. Sponsored by nation-states, these groups execute long-term, covert operations aimed at intelligence gathering, surveillance, or sabotage. In the dynamic realm of cybersecurity, OSINT becomes a critical tool in unmasking and understanding the operations of these elusive adversaries.

What are APTs?

An APT involves highly skilled hackers using complex techniques to penetrate networks and computers, They differ from regular hackers by their persistence, remaining hidden within a network for long periods. The *threat* aspect highlights their intent to cause harm or steal critical data, targeting business or government information, or disrupting the operations of the organizations they infiltrate.

How OSINT helps

OSINT experts start by scouring the internet for any pieces of information these APTs might have left behind. It's not just about looking at what's obvious; it's about finding the hidden messages in the vast sea of online data. For example, they might find a strangely registered domain name that doesn't seem to belong to any legitimate company or a series of posts on a hacker forum that hint at a planned cyber attack. These little pieces are like clues left at a crime scene, and they are crucial in piecing together the APT's identity.

Connecting the dots to reveal the big picture

The next step is like putting together a giant puzzle. This is where OSINT experts shine. They take each piece of information and start connecting them. Think of it as a detective's board, with strings connecting different clues across the web. For instance, an unusual login attempt from a foreign country, combined with a leaked document found on a different website, might point toward a specific APT's activity. By connecting these dots, OSINT experts can start to see patterns and strategies used by APTs. It's a meticulous and careful process, requiring a lot of patience and attention to detail.

Tracking digital footprints: a cyber chase

Even the stealthiest of APTs leave footprints in the digital world. These footprints are subtle, but they're there – in the form of digital records, transaction logs, or even slight irregularities in network traffic. OSINT experts use various methods to track these footprints. They might analyze server logs to see if there's unusual activity, or they could look at the metadata of a hacked document to find out when and where it was created. Each of these footprints is a valuable clue in understanding not just who the APTs are, but also how they operate.

The bigger picture: understanding context

One of the most important parts of OSINT is not just collecting data, but understanding the context around it. This means looking at the *why* and *how* of APT activities.

For example, if a certain APT is targeting energy companies, OSINT experts would try to figure out why. Is there a political motive? Is it about disrupting a country's energy supply? Understanding this framework helps in predicting future targets and motives of APTs.

Real cases of APTs

Let's look at some real examples where OSINT helped or could have helped in catching these cyber spies:

- **Stuxnet attack**: This was a big deal back in 2010. A computer worm called Stuxnet was used to damage Iran's nuclear program. It was really advanced and is believed to have been made by a country whose identity still isn't known as of 2023. By looking at how this worm was built, experts used OSINT to figure out how Stuxnet worked, who was the target, and how much damage it could cause.

- **2016 DNC hack**: In this case, hackers got into the Democratic National Committee's emails. By checking the digital clues left behind, such as where the hackers' emails came from and the kind of malware they used, OSINT experts helped point out that a Russian APT group was likely responsible.

- **MGM Resorts International's hack**: A hacking group known as **Scattered Spider** targeted MGM Resorts International in 2023, leading to a shutdown of some casino and hotel computer systems across the U.S. This cyber attack affected several MGM-owned casinos and hotels, including the

Bellagio and the Cosmopolitan. The ransomware attack forced these properties to cease using their computers entirely, drastically impacting their operations. Now, as of November 2023, we're still not *fully* aware of the damage that was caused, but I promise security researchers are using OSINT tools and techniques to continue to investigate this attack.

Looking ahead, it's evident just from these examples that cyber threats will only become more complex. To stay ahead, security experts must keep using OSINT, adapt to new challenges, and tirelessly pursue those who threaten our online safety.

Combining OSINT with internal security

When it comes to melding OSINT with internal security systems, envision a detective meticulously piecing together clues from various sources. At the heart of this process is correlation, which is crucial for effective cybersecurity. Let's explore how to blend OSINT with internal security frameworks to boost cybersecurity defenses:

- **Integration with SIEM systems: Security Information and Event Management** (**SIEM**) systems are designed to provide a holistic view of an organization's security posture by collecting and analyzing data from various sources. When integrated with OSINT, these systems can gain an additional layer of context, enhancing their ability to detect and respond to threats. For example, imagine your SIEM system detects an unusual spike in network traffic from a specific geographic location. On its own, this might be a cause for concern, but not necessarily indicative of a cyber attack. However, when correlated with OSINT, which reveals recent cyber threats or activities originating from that same location, the SIEM system can more accurately assess the risk and trigger appropriate security protocols.

- **Synergy with EDR systems: Endpoint Detection and Response** (**EDR**) systems focus on identifying and managing threats on network endpoints. The integration of OSINT can significantly bolster an EDR's capabilities, particularly in identifying and understanding new or evolving threats. *How?* you might ask. Let's consider an EDR system that identifies a new form of malware on a company laptop. While the EDR can contain and eliminate the threat, integrating OSINT can provide insights into the origin and nature of the malware. Perhaps there's an ongoing campaign using this malware, as indicated by OSINT sources such as cybersecurity forums or threat intelligence feeds. This information can guide the security team in fortifying defenses against similar future attacks.

- **Combining SIEM and EDR with OSINT for proactive defense**: The true power of integrating OSINT with internal security tools lies in moving from a reactive to a proactive security posture. By leveraging the vast amount of publicly available information, organizations can anticipate and prepare for potential threats before they strike.

For example, a SIEM system, armed with OSINT, might detect chatter on dark web forums about a planned attack on organizations in your industry. This intelligence allows the security team to preemptively tighten security measures and monitor for specific attack signatures. Concurrently, the EDR system can be updated with this intelligence to watch for any early signs of compromise on endpoints.

Crafting a well-informed cybersecurity strategy

Now, how does this correlation translate into a robust cybersecurity strategy? It's about being both reactive and proactive. You're not just waiting for alarms to go off; you're anticipating where and how the next cyber attack might occur. By combining the insights from OSINT about emerging threats and trends with the real-time data from your internal systems, you get a 360-degree view of your cybersecurity landscape.

This combined approach enables you to craft strategies that are not only responsive to current threats but also anticipatory of future risks. For example, if OSINT reveals a rise in ransomware attacks targeting your industry, you can proactively fortify your defenses against this specific threat. Simultaneously, your internal data might help you identify vulnerabilities within your system that could be potential entry points for such attacks.

Continuous learning and adaptation in cybersecurity

Cyber threats are constantly evolving, and so should your cybersecurity strategies. Regular training and upskilling are non-negotiable for cybersecurity professionals. Staying updated on the latest tools, techniques, and threat landscapes is crucial.

Engaging with the cybersecurity community through forums and groups offers an additional layer of learning. These platforms are valuable for exchanging insights, discussing new threats, and learning from others' experiences. By staying connected and informed, cybersecurity professionals can continuously refine their strategies, ensuring they're always several steps ahead of potential cyber threats.

Cyber threat intelligence platforms and OSINT integration

Cyber threat intelligence platforms are the high-tech watchtowers of the digital world. They're tools that cybersecurity teams use to stay informed about potential cyber threats. Their job is to collect loads of information from all over the internet, analyze it, and then tell you what you need to know about possible cyber threats. They help organizations understand and prepare for attacks before they happen.

These platforms are not just about collecting data; they do a lot more:

- **Gathering data**: They scan various sources such as blogs, news sites, and even less traveled parts of the internet. They look for anything that might be a sign of a cyber threat, such as suspicious malware or hints of a cyber attack.

- **Analyzing in real time**: Imagine a super-smart system that can read and understand all this data almost as soon as it comes in. That's what these platforms do. They use special technology to quickly analyze the information and figure out whether there's a threat. Here are a couple of key techniques these types of systems could use:

- **Machine learning**: These platforms often use machine learning algorithms to analyze patterns in data. Machine learning enables them to learn from past incidents, improving their ability to identify and predict new types of cyber threats. For instance, by analyzing historical data, the platform can identify anomalies that deviate from normal patterns, suggesting potential cyber threats.

- **Signature detection**: Signature detection is a more traditional but still crucial technique. It involves scanning incoming data for known threat signatures—digital fingerprints of viruses, malware, and other malicious entities. This method is particularly effective for identifying and stopping known threats.

- **Sending alerts**: If they find something risky, such as a new virus or an ongoing cyber attack, they immediately send out warnings. This helps cybersecurity teams take action fast.

- **Connecting with other tools**: These platforms are team players. They work with other cybersecurity tools, such as firewalls and antivirus software, to make sure all parts of an organization's network are protected from threats.

Some big names in the game

Let's take a look at some of the well-known cyber threat intelligence platforms:

- **Trellix (formally FireEye)** (`https://www.trellix.com/platform/`): This platform is famous for spotting and dealing with complex cyber threats.

- **IBM X-Force Exchange** (`exchange.xforce.ibmcloud.com`): This is more like a community center where cybersecurity experts from all over the world share information about threats. Sharing is caring folks!

- **CrowdStrike Falcon X** (`crowdstrike.com/falcon-platform`): This site is a blend of automation and human intelligence. It not only uses technology to identify threats but also relies on experts to provide insights.

- **Recorded Future** (`recordedfuture.com`): OK, folks, this is my personal favorite! This platform is like a fortune teller for cybersecurity. It looks at tons of data to predict future threats, helping organizations to be ready for what's coming. Plus, they have a ton of great free resources for security research.

OSINT plays a major role in these platforms. The OSINT data collected by these types of platforms is then used to make their threat analysis tools even more powerful, giving a wider and more complete picture of potential cyber threats. Ah, *now* you're catching on to how powerful OSINT really is, huh?

Incorporating OSINT data into threat intelligence workflows

Open source intelligence serves a vital role in protecting organizations from ever-evolving cyber threats. By using publicly available data, security teams can gain invaluable insights to strengthen defensive plans. However, integrating OSINT into existing systems requires a thoughtful strategy to extract meaningful signals from a sea of noise.

I get asked all the time *"Dale, as a digital cowboy, how would you incorporate OSINT into threat intel?"* Well, first know that every company is different, but overall this is how I would focus my integration:

1. First up, define your quest! Outline your goals clearly before saddling up. Wrangling industry threats or investigating an attack? Different beasts and partners. This could involve using threat modeling frameworks to identify potential threats based on your industry, size, and digital footprint. These frameworks help in categorizing and prioritizing threats based on their likelihood and potential impact.

2. Next, we round up facts from across the web range – public forums, security sites, sneaky honeypots. But not all sources are created equal, so brand what holds weight. To collect data, you might employ web crawlers to systematically browse the web and gather information. Tools such as Shodan can scan for internet-connected devices, while others might scrape data from public forums and social media. Implementing APIs from various security platforms can automate the collection of threat feeds.

3. Then, we groom the data so it's primed for the rodeo. Deduplication removes redundant data, while normalization standardizes the format for easier analysis. Adding context might involve tagging data with metadata, such as source reliability and relevance to your specific threat model. We're shaping up nicely!

4. Now, to make connections and uncover patterns so we can wrangle this beast! Linking clues to spy campaigns, analyzing trends to expect threats, and even attribution to call out varmints behind attacks. Machine learning models can be trained to identify outliers or suspicious patterns in the data that might indicate emerging threats. Network analysis tools can also be used to link different pieces of information, revealing potential threat actors or attack methods. Pretty slick work, buddy!

5. Armed with insights, let's circle back and share with the homestead so we can all guard against threats. Sharing insights with your team involves using collaboration tools and possibly integrating your findings into existing security systems. Collecting feedback can be structured through regular meetings or digital platforms, allowing for continuous refinement of your intelligence processes. Personally, I'll take the feedback to heart and keep refining my processes.

6. Finally, we put this intelligence to work like a trusty sheepdog. This may include configuring firewalls to block known malicious IPs, adjusting spam filters to catch new phishing attempts, or updating security awareness training for staff based on the latest threat trends. You know, doing all you can to help keep the predators away!

7. We'll review regularly and I'll tap new tools to automate the busy work while staying up to date on enemy tricks. And with some cross-ranch collaboration, we'll be the best cyber wranglers in the West!

8. So mount up, partner! Together we'll protect this here enterprise from all manner of cyber bandits and rustlers with some downright impressive threat intel. Now let's ride!

Think of sharing OSINT intelligence like telling your neighbors about a suspicious car you saw. By sharing what you know, everyone can be more careful and safe. In the cyber world, if you find out about a possible threat or a new hacking trick, telling others helps them protect themselves too.

Sharing OSINT-derived intelligence with other platforms and teams

It's important to choose how you share this info and with whom.

Let's first tackle the whom:

- **Internal teams**: These are the people within your organization who handle IT and security. They need detailed, technical information to effectively respond to threats. This group typically appreciates the specifics, such as the type of malware, methods of attack, and technical IoCs. Sharing detailed threat intelligence with them helps in crafting precise defense mechanisms.

- **Other departments**: Not everyone in your company will understand or need to know the technical details of a cyber threat. For example, your marketing or sales teams should be informed about potential threats, but in a way that's clear and straightforward. You might say, *"There's a phishing scam going around pretending to be from a client. Please double-check any unusual requests for information or payments."*

- **External platforms**: These are specialized forums or digital spaces where cybersecurity professionals from different organizations share and discuss intelligence. Platforms such as ThreatConnect (`threatconnect.com`) or IBM X-Force Exchange (which we talked about just a few pages back) are examples. Here, the exchange of information isn't just about staying informed; it's about contributing to a collective defense against cyber threats. When using these platforms, it's important to share enough detail to be helpful but not so much that it could lead to additional vulnerabilities.

Tailoring your message:

- **To tech teams**: This group needs the full picture, including technical data such as suspicious IP addresses, domain names, or file hashes associated with a cyber threat. This level of detail allows them to set up the right defenses, such as adjusting firewalls or updating antivirus software to recognize new threats.

- **To non-tech people**: Simplify the information. The goal is to make them aware without overwhelming them with jargon. For instance, if there's a risk of email-based attacks, advise them on what to look out for in simple terms, such as, *"Be wary of emails that ask for sensitive information and don't click on links from unknown sources."*

Sharing relevant info quickly

Cybersecurity is a fast-moving field, and threats can evolve quickly. Sharing information quickly ensures that your team can act before the threat spirals or changes.

Make sure what you're sharing is directly relevant to the audience. If the information isn't directly impactful or actionable for the person receiving it, it might be better to leave it out. Overloading people with too much information, or info that isn't useful for them, can lead to important details being missed.

When sharing intelligence, especially on external platforms, be careful with sensitive details. Always consider the balance between sharing useful information and protecting sensitive data. For example, sharing that a specific type of attack is on the rise is helpful; sharing the specifics of your organization's vulnerabilities is not.

Encourage two-way exchange. When you share intelligence, invite feedback and additional information. This can provide new insights and help refine your understanding of the threat. It's like working on a group project where everyone's input can lead to a better outcome.

By sharing what you know about cyber threats, you're not just helping your team or company, but you're part of a bigger team working together to keep the internet safe. Remember, in cyber security, sharing what you know makes everyone stronger.

Building an OSINT-driven cyber threat intelligence program

In this part of our journey into OSINT, we're going to explore a crucial aspect: building a **Cyber Threat Intelligence** (**CTI**) program with OSINT. This may sound a bit like spy stuff, but it's actually quite straightforward. We first need to understand our requirements.

What are intelligence requirements?

These requirements are crucial in cybersecurity. It's about hyper-focusing on the information that will be most useful for an organization's security. Let's say you're in charge of cybersecurity for a company. The first question you'd ask is, *"What information do we need to protect ourselves?"* The answer to this question is your intelligence requirements. For a cybersecurity professional, this means being able to recognize and respond to the most pressing threats more efficiently.

Identifying key information needs

Now, the big question is: how do you figure out what information you need? This part can be unique for each organization. A gaming company, for example, might be most concerned about protecting its game servers and player data. A retail store, on the other hand, might focus more on securing customer transaction data.

The key here is specificity. It's not enough to say, "*We need to keep our network secure.*" You need to be precise. What aspects of the network? Are there specific types of attacks you're most vulnerable to? The more specific you are, the better you can tailor your cybersecurity efforts.

It's also essential to ensure that these intelligence requirements line up with what the organization is trying to achieve overall. For instance, if a company is most concerned about data breaches, its cybersecurity efforts should be heavily focused on preventing those.

The role of OSINT

OSINT acts as a powerful lens that helps focus on specific, relevant data amidst an ocean of information. Cybersecurity professionals use OSINT to monitor publicly available data sources, such as social media, forums, blogs, and news websites, to gather insights about potential threats. This information can range from the latest malware trends being discussed in hacker forums to data breaches reported in the news. By leveraging OSINT, cybersecurity professionals can stay ahead of potential threats and take proactive measures to protect their organizations. *How?* you ask. Let's break it down.

Maturity matters

The usage of OSINT varies significantly depending on the maturity level of an organization. For new entities, OSINT might simply mean keeping up to date with industry news and trends. As organizations evolve, their approach to OSINT becomes more structured and integral to their overall security posture. Mature organizations typically will have dedicated teams and some pretty cool tools to manage and analyze open source data. These teams utilize OSINT not just for situational awareness but also for predictive analytics, trend analysis, and even for anticipating and modifying likely threats.

Integrating internal and external data

It's essential to integrate findings from OSINT with internal data sources. This could include security logs, incident reports, and employee feedback. Combining these data sources provides a comprehensive view of your cybersecurity landscape.

Your CTI program should include continuous monitoring of both internal and external sources. Stay abreast of the latest developments in the cyber world and update your intelligence database regularly to ensure that your information is current and relevant.

Building a diverse and skilled team

Your CTI team is the backbone of your program. It should consist of individuals with diverse skills and backgrounds. You need cybersecurity experts, data analysts, researchers, and even individuals with a knack for psychology to understand hacker motives. Take the following into consideration as you build your teams:

- It's important to keep the skills of your team up to date and constantly evolving. Encourage continuous learning and professional development by organizing regular training sessions and workshops, and attending cybersecurity conferences. This will help keep your team sharp and informed.

- Create a collaborative environment where team members can share ideas and insights. Foster a culture of innovation where team members are encouraged to think outside the box and develop new methods for gathering and analyzing data.

- To enhance your CTI program, it's important to have the right set of tools. This includes software for data collection and analysis, threat intelligence platforms, and cybersecurity monitoring tools. Choose tools that are scalable, user-friendly, and offer comprehensive features that align with your objectives.

- Sometimes, off-the-shelf tools might not meet all your specific needs. Be prepared to develop custom solutions. This could involve creating bespoke software for data analysis or developing unique algorithms for threat detection.

When you're building a CTI program using OSINT, remember you start by figuring out what specific information your organization needs for its cybersecurity.

So, that's the scoop on mixing threat intelligence with open source intelligence. It's about smartly combining your security data with public info, choosing the right tools, and always being ready to learn and adapt. Remember, staying safe online is all about being informed and working together.

Case study: OSINT in a real-world cybersecurity incident

In July 2020, Twitter experienced a significant security breach where high-profile accounts were compromised and used to perpetrate a Bitcoin scam. The accounts of notable figures and organizations, including Barack Obama, Elon Musk, Jeff Bezos, and Apple, were hijacked to promote a cryptocurrency scam (`https://www.theverge.com/22163643/twitter-hack-bitcoin-scam-july-2020-elon-musk`).

The attack began with a phishing operation targeting Twitter employees. The attackers conducted a spear-phishing attack via phone, targeting specific Twitter employees with access to internal tools.

The attackers posed as representatives from Twitter's IT department and convinced employees to reveal their credentials. This successful social engineering tactic provided them with access to Twitter's internal systems.

After the attack, OSINT played a critical role in understanding the breach's nature. Researchers and cybersecurity experts used publicly available data, such as domain registration information and IP address analysis, to trace the origin of the scam messages.

Analysis of the cryptocurrency wallet addresses posted in the scam tweets, cross-referencing with blockchain transaction data available publicly, helped in mapping out the flow of the scammed funds. OSINT tools were used to monitor the spread and impact of the scam on social media platforms. This helped in rapidly understanding the scope of the attack. Twitter's response included locking down affected accounts, removing the scam tweets, and temporarily restricting verified accounts' ability to tweet.

OSINT continued to play a role in the post-incident analysis, helping to identify the attackers' tactics and prevent similar attacks in the future. This incident highlighted the importance of employee training against social engineering and the need for robust internal security measures. It also underscored the value of OSINT in both real-time response and post-incident analysis.

The Twitter hack of 2020 serves as a prominent example of how sophisticated phishing and social engineering attacks can lead to significant security breaches. It demonstrates the critical role of OSINT in quickly identifying, responding to, and learning from cyber threats. This incident underscores the need for continuous vigilance and improvement in cybersecurity practices. Now do you see how OSINT can help us with CIT?

Summary

In this chapter, we've journeyed from theoretical discussions of OSINT to its practical applications in cybersecurity. By covering the integration of threat intelligence and OSINT, the role of OSINT in identifying cyber threats, and how it enhances cybersecurity through real-world case studies, we've equipped you with the knowledge to utilize OSINT effectively. This newfound understanding enables you to identify potential threats with a combination of digital expertise and critical insight, applying these skills across the vast landscape of cybersecurity where human interaction is pivotal.

Next, we'll look at how we can protect our personal and organizational intel from cyber threats.

7

Protecting Your Identity and Organization from Cyber Threats

In a world where our lives are increasingly online, keeping our digital identity and our organizations safe from cyber threats is more important than ever. This chapter is all about learning how to protect ourselves in the digital world. We'll explore how the information we can find openly can be a powerful tool in this fight. By reading this chapter, you will gain insights into how publicly available information can be a double-edged sword, capable of compromising or safeguarding digital identities and organizational assets. This exploration will sharpen your skills in utilizing **Open Source Intelligence (OSINT)**, not just as a concept, but as a practical tool in your cyber defense arsenal.

We will cover the following main topics in this chapter:

- Understanding the role of OSINT in protecting your identity and organization
- Personal digital hygiene and OSINT
- Assessing and strengthening organizational security with OSINT
- Identifying and responding to cyber threats
- Investigating cyber incidents and breaches
- Building a resilient cyber defense with OSINT

Now, this chapter will take you quite deep in your understanding, but you should be able to handle it if you haven't skipped any chapters so far! Let's get going.

Understanding the role of OSINT in protecting your identity and organization

Welcome to this chapter all about keeping you and your organization safe from online dangers. OSINT has emerged as a critical tool in this ongoing battle. OSINT involves the collection and analysis of publicly available data to gather intelligence and inform decision-making. This data can come from various sources, including news reports, public records, social media, and more.

The role of OSINT in cybersecurity is complex. For individuals, OSINT can be helpful in protecting personal identities online. In an age where digital footprints are vast and often publicly accessible, being aware of what information *about you* is available online is crucial. OSINT techniques can help identify areas of vulnerability in your digital presence, such as exposed personal information, and guide you in taking steps to secure it.

For organizations, OSINT is vital for protecting against a range of cyber threats. It assists in identifying vulnerabilities in our digital infrastructure, understanding the tactics of potential attackers, and staying informed about the latest threats. OSINT can also be used to monitor mentions of the organization's online presence, providing insights into potential reputation risks and opportunities for engagement.

The advantages of proactive OSINT research for cybersecurity

Proactive OSINT research offers several advantages within cybersecurity. Firstly, it enables early identification of threats. By continuously monitoring various open sources, organizations can detect potential threats before they materialize into actual attacks. This early detection is crucial for implementing timely countermeasures.

Another advantage of proactive OSINT research is its role in threat intelligence. It helps organizations understand the broader context of cyber threats, including the motivations and methods of threat actors. This understanding is key to developing effective defense strategies.

Proactive OSINT also aids in risk management. By continually assessing the threat landscape, organizations can adjust their cybersecurity strategies to align with evolving threats. This dynamic approach to cybersecurity ensures that defenses remain relevant and robust.

Furthermore, being proactive with any aspect of cybersecurity is a much better stance than being reactive. I look at it as a form of *job security*.

Personal digital hygiene and OSINT

Your digital footprint is a trail of data you leave online. It includes social media activity, forum posts, digital transactions, and any online records. This includes not just the use of your computer – just think about how much data you put out because of that mobile device in your hands!

Tools such as data aggregators, search engines, and specialized software can scour the internet to compile a thorough picture of your digital footprint. This examination of data helps in identifying potentially risky behaviors or exposures. For example, sharing too much personal information on social media can make you an easy target for identity theft or social engineering attacks. By regularly reviewing your digital footprint, you can make informed decisions about your online activities and reduce your vulnerability to cyber threats.

Identifying and mitigating risks from your online presence

Once you have a clear understanding of your digital footprint, the next step is to mitigate any risks associated with it. This involves tightening privacy settings on social media, being cautious about the information you share online, and regularly reviewing your online accounts for any signs of unauthorized access or unusual activities.

The following are a few best practices for risk mitigation:

- **Audit your online presence**: Regularly conduct an audit of your online accounts and social media profiles. Check the information you have shared publicly and assess its sensitivity. Could this information be used against you in any way (e.g., for identity theft, social engineering, etc.)? Here's a couple of tools that can help organizations with this:

  - **Sprout Social** (`https://www.sproutsocial.com/`): A comprehensive tool for social media auditing, analytics, and management

  - **Hootsuite** (`https://www.hootsuite.com/`): This tool is for managing multiple social media accounts and tracking their performance

  - **Google Analytics** (`https://analytics.google.com/`): Essential for tracking and analyzing your website's performance

- **Tighten your privacy settings**: On social media platforms such as Facebook, Twitter, Instagram, and LinkedIn, review and adjust your privacy settings to limit who can see your posts, contact information, and profile details.

- **Google yourself**: Use search engines to see what information about you is publicly accessible.

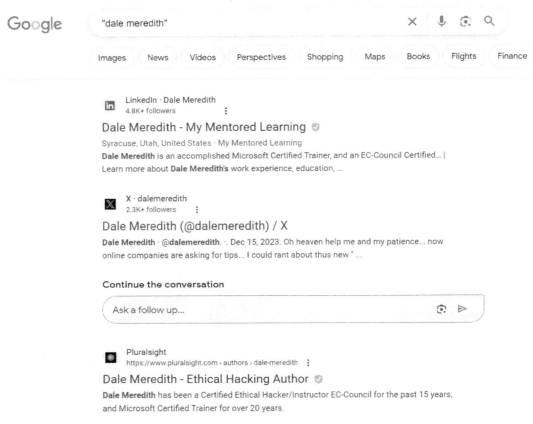

Figure 7.1 – Google yourself or your company to see what's exposed

Searching your name, email addresses, and phone numbers can reveal what a potential attacker can find.

- **Review and remove unnecessary information**: If you find sensitive information about yourself online (e.g., on old blogs, forums, or social media posts), take steps to remove it. Contact the website administrators if necessary.

The following are tools you can use to manage your online presence:

- **Google Alerts** (https://www.google.com/alerts): Set up alerts for your name and other personal identifiers.

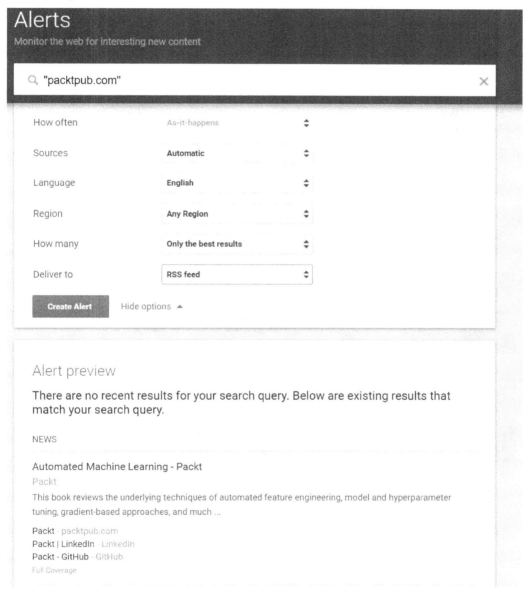

Figure 7.2 – Google Alerts can notify you when your search results update

This tool notifies you whenever new information containing these identifiers appears online. I have my name being monitored via this tool and it has saved my bacon on several occasions.

- **Have I Been Pwned?** (`https://haveibeenpwned.com/`): This site is run by my mate, Troy Hunt. Here you can check if your email addresses have been part of any data breaches. This helps in understanding potential exposures and taking steps such as changing passwords or enhancing account security. Make sure you hit the **Notify Me** button and this site will email you as soon as your email account is detected in a breach.

- **Privacy settings and tools on social media platforms**: Most social media platforms offer tools and settings to control your privacy. Train yourself with these options and use them to manage your online visibility. Note that these platforms change their features continually, so keep abreast of their changes by monitoring their press releases.

- **Data removal request services**: For information that cannot be removed manually, services such as DeleteMe (`https://joindeleteme.com/`) can assist in removing personal information from the internet by contacting data brokers and websites on your behalf.

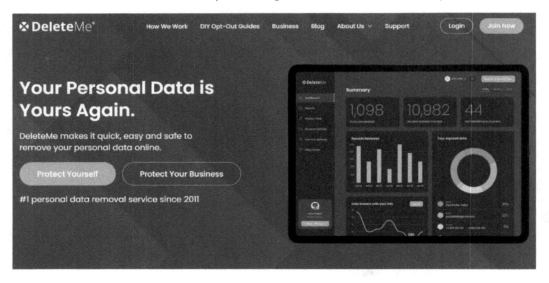

Figure 7.3 – Joindeleteme.com can help you manage your personal data online

DeleteMe is really a great service/tool to investigate, but it is kind of pricey. But can you really put a price on your privacy?

- **Stay informed**: Keep up to date with the latest trends in online privacy and security. This includes understanding new methods used by cybercriminals and staying aware of new tools and services that can protect your digital identity.

- **Educate yourself about phishing and social engineering**: Learn how to identify phishing attempts and social engineering tactics. This knowledge is critical in avoiding scams that could compromise your personal information. The easiest way to learn about phishing and social engineering is to jump over to YouTube and check out this great video from DefCon: `https://www.youtube.com/watch?v=jfXwdH-fkLE`. This presentation is by Chris Pritchard, a ground-breaking pentester.

By taking these steps and utilizing available tools, individuals can significantly reduce the risks associated with their online presence. This proactive approach to digital hygiene not only protects personal information but also reduces your overall vulnerability to cyber threats.

Enhancing your privacy and security

In addition to monitoring and mitigating risks, enhancing your overall privacy and security online is crucial. This includes using strong, unique passwords for different accounts. A strong password should be long, involve a mix of letters, numbers, and symbols, and shouldn't be something easy to guess such as your name, birthday, or anything that can be determined via OSINT (hobbies, sports teams, etc). We also want to remember the golden rule of passwords: *Longer is better*. Also, don't use the same password everywhere. I highly recommend using a password manager program to help with this. Also make sure to enable two-factor authentication on any accounts that offer it as a feature, and keep up to date with the latest phishing and scamming techniques.

OSINT tools can help identify potential vulnerabilities in your online behavior or digital assets. For example, they can reveal if your personal information is present on any data breach databases, or if your email address is being used for spamming.

Finally, it's essential to implement best practices for digital hygiene. This includes regularly updating your software to patch security vulnerabilities, being cautious about the apps and services you use, and educating yourself about the latest cybersecurity threats and how to avoid them. Personally, the growth of **Artificial Intelligence** (**AI**) scares me. As deepfakes and GenAI continue to change our world, know that just like any other technology, hackers will find a way to use that technology against you. So add AI to your list of things to research.

Assessing and strengthening organizational security with OSINT

An organization's cybersecurity posture is only as strong as its weakest link. External infrastructure, which includes web-facing assets such as websites, email servers, and cloud services, often presents multiple vectors for cyber attacks. Understanding and enhancing these aspects of your organization's digital presence is *critical*. OSINT plays a vital role in this endeavor, allowing for a complete analysis of probable vulnerabilities and threat vectors.

The process of assessing and strengthening your networks involves identifying vulnerabilities in web applications, email servers, DNS configurations, and other public-facing assets, and then implementing measures to mitigate these risks.

Identifying potential vulnerabilities

Here's a quick list of tools that should be used to identify any vulnerabilities in your infrastructure:

- **Web applications and websites**: Web-facing applications are often the first point of attack. Tools such as Nikto2 (https://cirt.net/Nikto2) can scan for over 7,000 vulnerabilities in web applications, including complex multi-level forms and password-protected areas.

```
┌──(kali㊸kali)-[~]
└─$ nikto -h scanme.nmap.org
- Nikto v2.5.0
─────────────────────────────────────────────
+ Multiple IPs found: 45.33.32.156, 2600:3c01::f03c:91ff:fe18:bb2f
+ Target IP:          45.33.32.156
+ Target Hostname:    scanme.nmap.org
+ Target Port:        80
+ Start Time:         2024-02-12 18:27:28 (GMT-7)
```

Figure 7.4 – Nikto scanning scanme.nmap.org

Its capability to prioritize full and incremental scans ensures comprehensive coverage.

- **Email servers**: Email systems are a common target for phishing and malware. Tools such as Vipre (https://vipre.com/) provide complete email security, guarding against viruses, ransomware, and identity theft, and include real-time threat intelligence for business protection.

- **Network security**: Securing the network infrastructure is crucial. Zeek (https://zeek. org/) operates passively, observing network traffic without interference. Zeek generates detailed transaction logs, file content, and outputs for security analysis.

```
root@debian12:/opt/zeek/logs/current# cat dns.log | zeek-cut id.orig_h query answers
10.0.2.15       -       -
10.0.2.15       httpredir.debian.org       debian.map.fastlydns.net,199.232.46.132
10.0.2.15       httpredir.debian.org       debian.map.fastlydns.net,2a04:4e42:48::644
10.0.2.15       _http._tcp.security.debian.org   debian.map.fastlydns.net
10.0.2.15
10.0.2.15
10.0.2.15
10.0.2.15
10.0.2.15       httpredir.debian.org       debian.map.fastlydns.net,199.232.46.132
10.0.2.15       httpredir.debian.org       debian.map.fastlydns.net,2a04:4e42:48::644
10.0.2.15       download.opensuse.org      195.135.221.134
10.0.2.15       download.opensuse.org      2001:67c:2178:8::13
root@debian12:/opt/zeek/logs/current#
```

Figure 7.5 – Zeek.org's open source monitoring tool allows you to passively see requests on your network

If you've been in the cybersecurity space for several years, you might remember another product called **Bro**. Well, Zeek is the recreation of that product. By default, Zeek provides over 60 log files, tracks 3,000+ network events, and has 10,000+ deployments worldwide. Its integration of DNS helps to prevent redirection attacks or traffic interception. Regular DNS analysis helps in identifying misconfigurations or unauthorized changes. Trust me, it's a cool tool.

- **Regular vulnerability scanning**: Continuous monitoring of digital assets using tools such as SecPod SanerNow (`https://www.secpod.com/`) can identify vulnerabilities and misconfigurations. Its patching feature and real-time vulnerability management ensure immediate and efficient remediation of identified risks.

- **Endpoint security**: Protecting endpoints from malware and other threats is critical. Malwarebytes (`https://www.malwarebytes.com/`) and many other companies offer endpoint security and incident response features such as anomaly detection, behavior matching, and real-time threat prevention.

A note about privacy and using online tools

Tools such as Nikto2, Vipre, Zeek, SecPod SanerNow, and Malwarebytes, when used correctly and with appropriate precautions, can provide valuable insights into your security posture without necessarily compromising privacy. The choice of tools for vulnerability assessment should be guided by a careful evaluation of security, privacy, and compliance requirements specific to your organization.

The digital world changes fast, and so do the ways hackers try to break in. We need to keep learning about new tools and ways to keep our digital house safe. Just like upgrading our devices and software, we need to apply the same processes to learning.

Identifying and responding to cyber threats such as ransomware

In today's digital age, the cyber threat landscape is constantly evolving, with ransomware emerging as a particularly insidious form of attack. Ransomware is a type of malicious software designed to block access to a computer system or data, typically by encrypting it, until a sum of money (ransom) is paid. This form of cyber attack has gained notoriety for its crippling effect on individual users, businesses, and even public infrastructure:

- **Key characteristics of ransomware**: Most ransomware variants encrypt the files on the victim's device, making them inaccessible. The attackers then demand a ransom for the decryption key. Payments are typically demanded in cryptocurrencies such as Bitcoin, making it difficult to trace the attackers.

  While early ransomware attacks were indiscriminate, recent trends show more targeted attacks against specific organizations, businesses, or public services, where the likelihood of a higher ransom payout is greater. Like other cyber threats, ransomware often gains access to systems through phishing emails that trick users into downloading the malware.

- **Impact of ransomware:** Beyond the ransom payment, victims often suffer significant financial losses due to operational disruptions, data loss, and reputational damage. Ransomware can paralyze entire systems, leading to significant operational challenges, especially in critical sectors such as healthcare and government services. Even if the ransom is paid, there's no guarantee that the data will be fully recovered or that the attackers haven't compromised the data.

- **Prevention and mitigation:** To combat ransomware, regular data backups, employee education on phishing, and maintaining up-to-date security measures are crucial. Regular backups ensure data recovery in case of an attack, while educating employees on the risks of phishing can prevent the initial malware infection. Keeping systems and software updated with the latest security patches can prevent attackers from exploiting known vulnerabilities. Having a robust incident response plan can also significantly minimize the impact of a ransomware attack.

- **Recent trends in ransomware:** Recent trends in ransomware indicate increasing sophistication, with attackers conducting extensive reconnaissance to target specific organizations or industries more effectively. A worrying development is the rise of *double extortion* tactics, where attackers not only encrypt the victim's data but also threaten to release sensitive information publicly if the ransom is not paid.

Detecting phishing and social engineering attempts

Detecting malware and ransomware using OSINT, this process involves a very proactive approach to cybersecurity. By monitoring hacker forums and dark web marketplaces, professionals can gain early warnings about new malware strains or cybercriminal campaigns. Threat intelligence feeds play a crucial role, offering real-time alerts on emerging threats. Analyzing phishing emails, which often serve as malware distribution channels, helps in identifying attack vectors. Additionally, scrutinizing file hashes, IP addresses, and URLs in public databases aids in recognizing known malicious entities. These OSINT methodologies empower cybersecurity teams to anticipate and mitigate potential threats, safeguarding digital assets effectively.

Examining uncertain URLs with OSINT technologies can provide valuable insights into their domain registration, standing, and any related criminal activity. In this procedure, resources such as WHOIS lookups are crucial because they reveal information about the domain owners and highlight any possible problems with authenticity.

Analysis of email headers is another important technique. Examining the email's header closely is required in order to spot irregularities or signs of email spoofing. Email header components such as the `Received:  from` line can provide important information about the email's origin, frequently including covert malevolent intent.

Social media analysis also plays a pivotal role in identifying social engineering threats. By analyzing social media profiles and posts, one can gather personal details, interests, or connections that could be exploited in targeted attacks. Similarly, regular monitoring of online platforms for any exposed employee information is essential in preventing social engineering attacks.

It's Exotic Lily story time

A great example of threat actors using OSINT techniques to spear-phish is what we learned from the hacking group Exotic Lily.

Exotic Lily has mastered spear-phishing. Spear-phishing is like fishing in a lake, but instead of catching all the fish, a fisherman targets a specific fish and hunts it with a speargun. Similarly, in spear-phishing, cyber attackers such as Exotic Lily don't send random emails to thousands of people. They choose a specific person or company and then create a special email just for them. This email looks real and trustworthy, often seeming to come from a friend, a boss, or a well-known company.

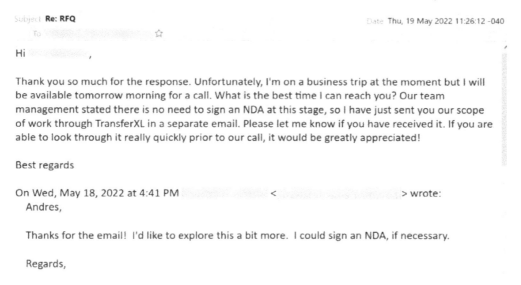

Figure 7.6 – A sample of one of Exotic Lily's emails

So, how does Exotic Lily do it? First, they do a lot of homework. They dig deep into their target's world. They might look at social media, company websites, and other public information to learn about the person or company they want to attack. This helps them make their fake emails very convincing.

Let me give you an example. Let's say Exotic Lily found out you're attending a cybersecurity conference, they might send an email that looks like it's from the conference organizers. This email could say something about a change in the schedule and ask you to click on a link for more details. But when you click that link, you unknowingly loaded malware onto your device. Once the malware is in, it can do a lot of damage. It might lock up your files and demand money to unlock them, or it could secretly watch everything you do on your computer and send that information back to the attackers.

Exotic Lily's spear-phishing emails are cleverly crafted. They'll use the right names, the right logos, and even the right kind of language to make you think it's a genuine email. They might even include small details about your life or work that you think nobody else knows. This is what makes their attacks so dangerous and hard to spot.

Understanding how Exotic Lily operates is key to protecting yourself. Remember, in the digital world, not everything is what it seems. Being cautious, especially with emails that ask you to click on links or download attachments, is your first line of defense. In the next sections, we'll dive into how you can defend against these attacks and keep your information safe.

The Cobalt Dickens group and their tricky spear-phishing attacks

Have you heard about the Cobalt Dickens group? They focus on tricking universities by sending emails that look super real. Imagine getting an email that looks like it's from your school's IT department, asking you to update your password. You'd probably think it's safe, right? That's what they count on.

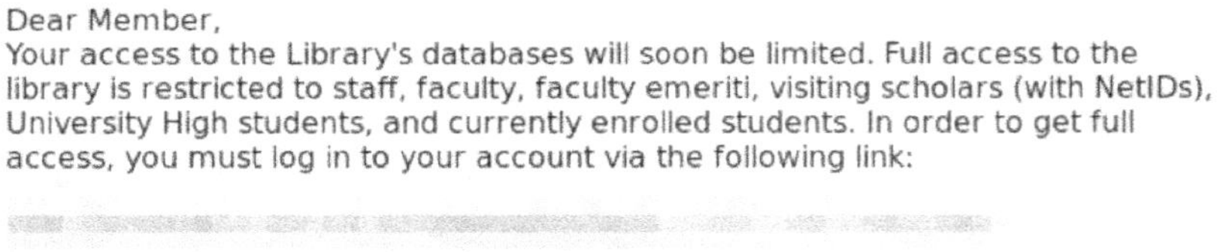

Dear Member,
Your access to the Library's databases will soon be limited. Full access to the library is restricted to staff, faculty, faculty emeriti, visiting scholars (with NetIDs), University High students, and currently enrolled students. In order to get full access, you must log in to your account via the following link:

Figure 7.7 – Cobalt Dickens phishing email

But here's the twist: they don't just stop at emails. They also create websites that look exactly like the ones you use at school. So, when you try to log in, thinking you're on the real site, you're actually giving your username and password straight to them.

The most interesting part? They use OSINT tools, making it harder for people to catch them. When Cobalt Dickens sneaks into a university's system, they can grab lots of important stuff. They're after the cool research and new ideas that universities work on. But that's not all. They can also get personal information about students and teachers, which is a big problem.

Understanding what groups like Cobalt Dickens and Exotic Lily do helps us stay one step ahead. It's like knowing the tricks of a magician. By learning about their sneaky methods, we can be better prepared and protect our organizations and ourselves from these folks. So, always be careful with your emails and where you log in – it's a big part of keeping those clever foxes out of our digital henhouse!

Investigating cyber incidents and breaches

An essential part of responding to cyber incidents is conducting technical investigations into the affected websites. Responders can find possible vulnerabilities in websites by studying their technical characteristics with the use of OSINT tools. Website hosting information and SSL certificate details are only two of the many technical aspects that could be uncovered. An example of this is that you find a company website that is being hosted on a shared server known for security vulnerabilities. Using tools such as WHOIS or DomainTools, responders can identify the hosting provider and research known vulnerabilities associated with that provider. Likewise, tools such as SSL Labs' SSL Test (`https://www.ssllabs.com/ssltest/`) can be used to examine the SSL certificates of a website, revealing potential security gaps such as outdated encryption algorithms or certificates issued by non-trusted authorities.

SSL Report: daledumbsitdown.com

Assessed on: Wed, 31 Jan 2024 22:27:32 UTC | Hide | Clear cache

Scan Another >>

	Server	Test time	Grade
1	**2a02:4780:22:47ea:796f:cee5:a437:3c1a** Unable to connect to the server	Wed, 31 Jan 2024 22:26:21 UTC Duration: 15.476 sec	-
2	**154.41.250.227** Ready	Wed, 31 Jan 2024 22:26:36 UTC Duration: 56.303 sec	A

Figure 7.8 – SSLLabs.com tests the strength of your certificates

Investigating older versions of websites, such as those accessible through the Wayback Machine (`https://web.archive.org/`), can provide useful information. Information such as the contact details of senior management, which is commonly included in older versions of company websites, might be crucial for determining the extent of the breach.

Another important part of investigating a target website is finding its sub-domains. Private information, such VPN portals or server addresses, may be stored on these sub-domains. You can learn a lot about the target's network architecture by using Google search commands to find these sub-domains, as well as Shodan or Censys.

People frequently fail to properly research available resources, such as job postings and resumes. These may reveal information regarding the server OS, networking hardware, firewall configuration, and other aspects of an organization's IT system.

Also, sensitive company data that has been accidentally made public on public servers can be exposed with our OSINT tools. By analyzing their metadata, we can uncover previously unknown information about these files, such as the name of the creator, the program utilized, and the operating system of the device they were made on.

Uncovering the source, scope, and impact of cyber incidents

When responding to a cyber incident, having the right investigative tools is key to uncovering what happened. To understand the nature of the issue, investigators can use OSINT tools to analyze traffic patterns and establish what's *normal*. Any deviations from normal could suggest something sketchy is up. Looking for repeating patterns can also show if automated mechanisms such as malware are at play.

Spotting weird anomalies that don't fit expected system administration norms is also super useful. By carefully reviewing the collected data, investigators can catch errors or activities that seem off.

Gathering and studying host artifacts is another key piece of the puzzle. This includes stuff such as running processes, services, hashes of executables, and account activities. Each artifact provides insights into potential unauthorized access or changes.

For deeper analysis, investigators may look at unverified internet connections, PowerShell commands (for sneaky fileless attacks), and file processes that could signal data theft. User login patterns that seem strange could also indicate unauthorized access.

Network artifacts are equally important to examine. Investigators check out DNS traffic, remote access protocols, website access logs, and more for signs of shady access or data exfiltration.

When we're trying to figure out what happened in a cyber attack, we use two main ways to gather clues: digital forensics and OSINT. Think of digital forensics like being a detective who looks closely at the evidence on computers and networks. This includes checking the list of running programs, the activities of user accounts, and looking for any unusual connections to the internet. It's all about finding signs of sneaky access or stolen data.

OSINT is like being a detective who gathers information from sources that everyone can see, including news reports, websites, or social media. It's not about looking at the computers and networks that were attacked, but about collecting extra information from outside sources.

Both these methods are super important. While digital forensics helps us understand exactly what happened in a cyber attack, OSINT gives us more context and background information. It's like having two detectives working together – one looks at the crime scene, and the other talks to people and checks out different places to get more clues. By pursuing both of these avenues, we can get a full picture of the cyber attack and make our computer defenses stronger for the future.

Building a resilient cyber defense with OSINT

To identify the risks that might have the greatest impact on a company, OSINT is essential. Organizations can discover threat actors aiming at them, confidential data, published on public repositories, and credentials leaked by monitoring hazards across many online platforms, including the dark and clear web. With the use of OSINT, businesses can learn about their attack vectors and exposed assets, which improves their understanding of cybersecurity trends in general.

There are active and passive forms of OSINT:

- To gather passive OSINT, one can do things such as sign up for Google alerts regarding cybersecurity-related trends in one's industry.

- Active OSINT, on the other hand, necessitates more thorough collecting, such as breaking into dark web forums that demand special access, and hence provides a more complex picture of possible dangers.

But how does this tie into your organization? It's all about tailoring your findings to your organization's unique vulnerabilities. You align your findings with your organization's risk profile, understanding that what's a minor threat to one might be a critical vulnerability for another. This process isn't static; it's a continuous loop of monitoring, analyzing, and adjusting. It's like playing a high-stakes game of chess where every move is calculated and every piece is vital for your defense.

Collaborating with the cybersecurity community

Your next strategic move is collaboration. Sharing OSINT-derived insights with other organizations is akin to forming alliances in a battle against a common enemy. It's about creating a united front, where shared knowledge becomes a shared shield.

Participation in cybersecurity forums and industry-specific events is crucial. Here, you're not just a passive listener but an active contributor. Your insights from OSINT could be the missing piece in someone else's puzzle. These events are melting pots of ideas, strategies, and experiences. By engaging, you gain access to a broader spectrum of knowledge, which, in turn, fuels your own cybersecurity strategies. It's a symbiotic relationship where every shared insight fortifies the collective defense.

Adapting to the evolving threat landscape

The first step in adaptation is staying informed. Cyber threats evolve rapidly, and what was a cutting-edge defense strategy yesterday might be inadequate today. Keeping up to date with the latest trends and developments in cybersecurity is vital. Besides joining online forums, make sure you attend security seminars on a regular basis, read trade journals, and follow influential cybersecurity figures on social media:

- **Industry publications**: Regularly visit sites such as The Hacker News (`https://thehackernews.com/`) and Krebs on Security (`https://krebsonsecurity.com/`) for the latest in cybersecurity news. I monitor these almost daily.

The Hacker News

Home   Cyber Attacks   Vulnerabilities   Store   Contact

Glupteba Botnet Evades Detection with Undocumented UEFI Bootkit

📅 Feb 13, 2024   Cryptocurrency / Rootkit

The Glupteba botnet has been found to incorporate a previously undocumented Unified Extensible Firmware...

PikaBot Resurfaces with Streamlined Code and Deceptive Tactics

📅 Feb 13, 2024   Cyber Threat / Malware

The threat actors behind the PikaBot malware have made significant changes to the malware in what has been...

Midnight Blizzard and Cloudflare-Atlassian Cybersecurity Incidents: What to Know

📅 Feb 13, 2024   SaaS Security / Data Breach

The Midnight Blizzard and Cloudflare-Atlassian cybersecurity incidents raised alarms about the vulnerabilities inherent in...

Ivanti Vulnerability Exploited to Install 'DSLog' Backdoor on 670+ IT Infrastructures

📅 Feb 13, 2024   Vulnerability / Cyber Threat

Figure 7.9 – TheHackerNews.com is a great resource for keeping yourself in the "know"

- **Webinars and online training**: Platforms such as Pluralsight (`https://www.pluralsight.com/`) offer a wealth of learning resources that can help you stay sharp and informed. There's a really good author who has published over 30 courses there I'd highly recommend.

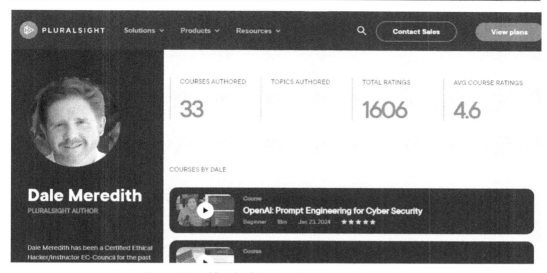

Figure 7.10 – Pluralsight.com – this author is amazing!

You also have conferences that you should be attending. I also personally attend Blackhat and Defcon each year in Las Vegas. You'll often find me in the training session.

- **Social media**: Follow cybersecurity experts on platforms such as LinkedIn or Twitter for real-time updates and insights. I know a guy who goes by `@dalemeredith` that you might want to follow!

Remember, in the world of cybersecurity, information is not just power—it's protection. Stay curious, stay informed, and stay one step ahead.

Updating your OSINT-driven cybersecurity strategy as needed

An OSINT-driven cybersecurity strategy is not a set-it-and-forget-it plan. It requires regular updates and adjustments based on the latest intelligence and trends. Here are a few key areas I'd focus on:

- **Reassessing risk profiles**: As your organization evolves, so do its vulnerabilities. Regularly reassess your risk profile based on the latest OSINT data.

- **Enhancing defensive measures**: Use insights from recent cyber incidents to strengthen your defenses. This could involve updating firewalls, enhancing network security, or training staff on new phishing tactics.

- **Leveraging new tools**: The OSINT tool landscape is always expanding. Stay on the lookout for new tools and technologies that can enhance your intelligence-gathering and analysis capabilities.

Don't forget the tools

When building a resilient cyber defense using OSINT, there are several tools and platforms that can be incredibly effective. In previous chapters, we've explored a variety of OSINT tools that are instrumental in building a strong cyber defense.

> **Note**
>
> Most of these tools are included with Kali Linux, Parrot, and Trace Labs, all of which are great OSINT-based platforms.

Let's revisit these tools with a focus on how you can access and utilize them:

- **Shodan** (`https://www.shodan.io/`): Known as the hacker's search engine, Shodan provides real-time data on internet-connected devices. Imagine you're investigating exposed databases. You could use Shodan to search for specific types of databases (e.g., MongoDB) that are publicly accessible. By entering a query such as `product:MongoDB`, Shodan lists MongoDB databases visible online. This search can reveal databases that may not be properly secured, highlighting potential vulnerabilities. Always ensure ethical use and legal compliance when conducting such searches.

- **Google Hacking Database** (`https://www.exploit-db.com/google-hacking-database`): By utilizing specific search queries listed in the database, such as `intitle:index.of` followed by a server version or a specific file type, you can discover publicly accessible directories that might contain sensitive data. This method helps identify potential data leaks or areas where a website's security could be enhanced. Always use this information responsibly and ethically.

- **Maltego** (`https://www.maltego.com/`): This tool excels in visual link analysis, helping to map networks and understand relationships between different digital entities. You might start by investigating a domain to understand its digital footprint. Begin by entering the domain name as your starting entity. Next, apply transformations to uncover related entities such as associated emails, subdomains, or social media links. This process visually maps out connections, offering insights into the domain's infrastructure and associated digital presence.

- **theHarvester**: You can find theHarvester on GitHub (`https://github.com/laramies/theHarvester`). This tool can be used to find email addresses, subdomains, and other data related to the domain in question. By executing a command in theHarvester with the target domain specified, it fetches and compiles a list of email addresses, subdomains, and potentially associated individuals or roles within the company. This information aids in cybersecurity analysis by revealing potential entry points or connections related to the target.

- **OSINT Framework** (`https://osintframework.com/`): While not a tool itself, It categorizes various OSINT tools based on the type of information you're seeking, such as domain data, people search, or social media analysis. This framework is designed to guide users to the right tools for their investigative needs, making it easier to gather intelligence from public sources. Note that this site is continually updating the link to new tools.

- **SpiderFoot** (`https://intel471.com/solutions/attack-surface-protection`): To utilize SpiderFoot for OSINT gathering, you'd start by setting up a scan targeting a specific entity, like a domain name or IP address. SpiderFoot automates the process of collecting a wide array of information related to the target, such as domain details, email addresses, and potential vulnerabilities. This tool streamlines the reconnaissance phase of cybersecurity assessments, making it easier to identify security risks.

- **Recon-ng** (`https://github.com/lanmaster53/recon-ng`): To use Recon-ng for OSINT, you'd typically select a module tailored to the type of data you're seeking, such as finding email addresses associated with a domain. After configuring the module with the necessary parameters, Recon-ng will execute the task, gathering data from various public sources. This tool is particularly useful for piecing together digital profiles of targets based on publicly available information.

- **TinEye** (`https://tineye.com/`): A reverse image search engine that's particularly useful for verifying the authenticity of an image or finding out whether it has appeared elsewhere on the web. You simply upload an image or enter a URL, and TinEye searches its database for matches or similar pictures. This tool is valuable for OSINT, especially in investigations related to digital media verification.

- **X Pro**, formally TweetDeck (`https://pro.twitter.com/`): This is used for real-time monitoring and analysis of Twitter feeds. It allows users to monitor Twitter feeds, track hashtags, mentions, and more, providing valuable insights into social media trends. This tool is particularly useful for OSINT purposes in tracking public sentiment, identifying trends, and gathering real-time information from Twitter.

- **Creepy** (`https://github.com/ilektrojohn/creepy`): A geolocation OSINT tool, Creepy aggregates location data from various social media platforms and maps out a person's movements based on their digital footprint. This tool is especially useful for investigations requiring an understanding of an individual's location patterns over time.

Even while these tools provide great potential for obtaining OSINT, it is essential to use them responsibly and ethically, following all applicable laws. Staying knowledgeable and up to date in the realm of cybersecurity is crucial, as the technologies at our disposal are always evolving along with the digital landscape.

Summary

To wrap up this chapter, we've learned how important it is to always keep up to date with cybersecurity. Using sources such as The Hacker News and Pluralsight helps us stay sharp. We must keep changing our cyber defense strategies to deal with new threats. Attending webinars and following experts online are great ways to learn more. Remember, in cybersecurity, being informed and ready to adapt is key to keeping your organization and yourself safe online.

Now you've read this book, I hope you've grasped the importance of OSINT. We started with the basics, examined a *plethora* of cool tools and techniques, and talked about staying safe and anonymous online. We saw how OSINT helps us find hidden cyber threats and protect ourselves and our organizations. It helps us stay one step ahead of hackers and keep our online world safe. It's a big part of fighting against online dangers.

Get this book's PDF version and more

Scan the QR code (or go to `packtpub.com/unlock`). Search for this book by name, confirm the edition, and then follow the steps on the page.

Note: Keep your invoice handy. Purchases made directly from Packt don't require an invoice.

Unlock Your Exclusive Benefits

Your copy of this book includes the following exclusive benefits:

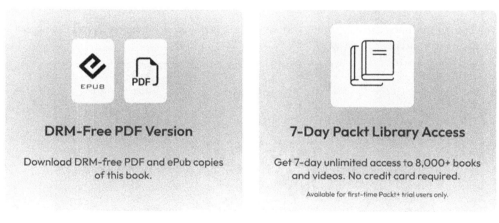

DRM-Free PDF Version

Download DRM-free PDF and ePub copies of this book.

7-Day Packt Library Access

Get 7-day unlimited access to 8,000+ books and videos. No credit card required.

Available for first-time Packt+ trial users only.

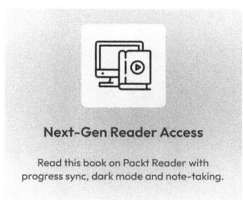

Next-Gen Reader Access

Read this book on Packt Reader with progress sync, dark mode and note-taking.

Follow the guide below to unlock them. The process takes only a few minutes and needs to be completed once.

Unlock this book's free benefits in 3 easy steps

Step 1

Keep your purchase invoice ready for *Step 3*. If you have a physical copy, scan it using your phone and save it as a PDF, JPG, or PNG.

For more help on finding your invoice, visit `https://www.packtpub.com/en-us/unlock?step=1`.

> **Note**
>
> If you bought this book directly from Packt, no invoice is required. After *Step 2*, you can access your exclusive content right away.

Step 2

Scan the QR code or go to `packtpub.com/unlock`.

On the page that opens (similar to *Figure 8.1* on desktop), search for this book by name and select the correct edition.

Unlock Your Book's Free Benefits

Bought a Packt book from Amazon or one of our channel partners? Unlock your free benefits in 3 easy steps.

Find Your Book   Sign Up or Sign In   Upload Purchase Proof

Need Help?

Search for your book here

1. Find Your Book

Q Search by title or ISBN

2. Sign up (Free) or Sign In

3. Upload Purchase Proof

Figure 8.1: Packt unlock landing page on desktop

Step 3

After selecting your book, sign in to your Packt account or create one for free. Then upload your invoice (PDF, PNG, or JPG, up to 10 MB). Follow the on-screen instructions to finish the process.

Need Help

If you get stuck and need help, visit https://www.packtpub.com/unlock-benefits/help for a detailed FAQ on how to find your invoices and more. This QR code will take you to the help page.

> **Note**
> If you are still facing issues, reach out to customercare@packt.com.

Index

packtpub.com

Subscribe to our online digital library for full access to over 7,000 books and videos, as well as industry leading tools to help you plan your personal development and advance your career. For more information, please visit our website.

Why subscribe?

- Spend less time learning and more time coding with practical eBooks and Videos from over 4,000 industry professionals

- Improve your learning with Skill Plans built especially for you

- Get a free eBook or video every month

- Fully searchable for easy access to vital information

- Copy and paste, print, and bookmark content

Did you know that Packt offers eBook versions of every book published, with PDF and ePub files available? You can upgrade to the eBook version at packtpub.com and as a print book customer, you are entitled to a discount on the eBook copy. Get in touch with us at customercare@packtpub.com for more details.

At www.packtpub.com, you can also read a collection of free technical articles, sign up for a range of free newsletters, and receive exclusive discounts and offers on Packt books and eBooks.

Other Books You May Enjoy

If you enjoyed this book, you may be interested in these other books by Packt:

Operationalizing Threat Intelligence

Kyle Wilhoit, Joseph Opacki

ISBN: 978-1-80181-468-3

- Discover types of threat actors and their common tactics and techniques
- Understand the core tenets of cyber threat intelligence
- Discover cyber threat intelligence policies, procedures, and frameworks
- Explore the fundamentals relating to collecting cyber threat intelligence
- Understand fundamentals about threat intelligence enrichment and analysis
- Understand what threat hunting and pivoting are, along with examples
- Focus on putting threat intelligence into production
- Explore techniques for performing threat analysis, pivoting, and hunting

Reconnaissance for Ethical Hackers

Glen D. Singh

ISBN: 978-1-83763-063-9

- Understand the tactics, techniques, and procedures of reconnaissance
- Grasp the importance of attack surface management for organizations
- Find out how to conceal your identity online as an ethical hacker
- Explore advanced open source intelligence (OSINT) techniques
- Perform active reconnaissance to discover live hosts and exposed ports
- Use automated tools to perform vulnerability assessments on systems
- Discover how to efficiently perform reconnaissance on web applications
- Implement open source threat detection and monitoring tools

Packt is searching for authors like you

If you're interested in becoming an author for Packt, please visit `authors.packtpub.com` and apply today. We have worked with thousands of developers and tech professionals, just like you, to help them share their insight with the global tech community. You can make a general application, apply for a specific hot topic that we are recruiting an author for, or submit your own idea.

Share your thoughts

Now you've finished *The OSINT Handbook*, we'd love to hear your thoughts! Scan the QR code below to go straight to the Amazon review page for this book and share your feedback or leave a review on the site that you purchased it from.

`https://packt.link/r/1837638276`

Your review is important to us and the tech community and will help us make sure we're delivering excellent quality content.

www.ingramcontent.com/pod-product-compliance
Lightning Source LLC
Chambersburg PA
CBHW080528060326
40690CB00022B/5060